THE HORSE IN ART

THE HORSE IN ART

John Baskett

Foreword by Paul Mellon

New York Graphic Society Boston

For Nicky and Samantha

International Standard Book Number: 0-8212-0757-1
Library of Congress Catalog Card Number: 79-89641

First published in England
by George Weidenfeld and Nicolson Ltd

First United States edition

Editor and Art Director: Mark Boxer
Designers: Tim Higgins and Andrew Kay
Picture Research: Jane Beamish
Text Editor: Martha Caute

New York Graphic Society books are published
by Little, Brown and Company

Printed and bound in Italy by Arnoldo Mondadori
Editore – Verona
Typeset in Monotype and Monophoto Baskerville
by Keyspools Ltd, Golborne, Lancs.

Slipcase illustrations
FRONT George Stubbs, ARA (1724–1806): *Horse attacked by a Lion*, 1769.
Reproduced by permission of the Tate Gallery, London (Photo: John Webb)
BACK Jean-Baptiste-Camille Corot (1796–1875): *A Horseman in a Wood*,
c. 1850–2. Reproduced by permission of the National Gallery, London

Author's Acknowledgements

I would particularly like to record my debt of gratitude to Paul
Mellon, who has not only allowed me the run of his
incomparable sporting collection, but who has also generously
written the Foreword to this book. Mr Mellon's interest and
patronage have been the leading factor in the promotion of
studies in British art over recent years, and I count myself very
fortunate to have been a recipient of his encouragement. My
special thanks go also to Beverly Carter, Mr Mellon's
Administrative Secretary, for patiently providing photographs
and listings. Richard Day, Dudley Snelgrove and Joan Bennet
have given much help, and Judy Egerton has kindly read the
typescript and made a number of valuable suggestions. I thank
Fiona Mills for typing my manuscript. I would like to
acknowledge the help of the following who, through their
published work and written communications, have given
assistance: Charles Chenevix Trench, John Clabby, Patricia
Connor, Brian Cook, John Couper, Anthony Dent, John
Fletcher, Myles Glover, Arthur Jones, Elaine Mann, Lionel
Lambourne, Roger Longrigg, William Latto, John von Stade,
Stella Walker and Reginald Williams. I would like also to thank
the Department of Greek and Roman Antiquities and the
Department of Prints and Drawings at the British Museum,
Messrs Arthur Ackermann, Thomas Agnew and Sons, the Paul
Mellon Centre for Studies in British Art, the National Museum
of Racing, Saratoga Springs, New York, and the Yale Center
for British Art, New Haven, Connecticut.

CONTENTS

Foreword by Paul Mellon   7

Introduction   21

The Horse in Ancient Civilizations   43

The Early Oriental Horse   50

The Medieval Horse and the Age of Chivalry   55

The Renaissance Masters   65

The Age of the Baroque   75

The Late Oriental Horse   85

The Eighteenth Century   88

The Nineteenth Century and the Modern World   117

List of Illustrations   156

Index   160

These few reflections on the horse in art have come to my mind while reviewing the many handsome illustrations presented in this book. They have given me extra pleasure while reading John Baskett's interesting history of the horse, and the horse's relationship to art. As an amateur of fox hunting and racing, I have naturally always been more drawn to representations of and descriptions of eighteenth- and nineteenth-century sporting scenes. However, I find this vast panorama of many centuries very stimulating, and it has given me a much broader perspective on the whole fascinating subject.

Persuaded to do so by both the author and the publishers, I have allowed myself the privilege of touching here and there on my own experiences during a long life both of riding horses and of collecting pictures; and, indeed, these activities are so much a part of me that I could not have done otherwise. I have been carried back by these pages not only to the best days of my childhood, to ponies and gymkhanas and paperchases, but also to my first forays into fox hunting, which later became a lifelong addiction. They have brought happy memories of racing in America and England. They make more meaningful a wartime stint as an officer candidate and then as an instructor at the US Cavalry School at Fort Riley. They have even reminded me of the toil and trauma of my still-pursued annual one-hundred-mile trail ride in the mountains of Virginia which, unlike what the poet said about poetry, is anything but 'emotion recollected in tranquillity'! The book also revived memories of the thrill of riding one's favourite hunter in point-to-points, of seeing one's steeplechaser winning that great timber classic, the Maryland Hunt Cup, and of living again those halcyon days when Mill Reef won the Gimcrack, the Derby, the Eclipse, the King George and Queen Elizabeth stakes, as well as that icing on the cake, the Arc de Triomphe at Longchamp. And of course, last but not least, it has reminded me of many happy years of collecting British sporting art.

John Skeaping, the eminent modern-animal sculptor once said, '. . . you can't talk about art – the more you talk about it the farther away from it you get.' On the other hand, talk about horses can be interesting and instructive if it doesn't drift into pathos and sentimentality. And if, as it is said, one picture is worth a thousand words, we can be sure that the contents of this volume, in addition to the author's instructive essay, will bring meaning, unexpected revelation and true emotional appeal to all who love the horse or who have a genuine appreciation of art.

There are so many ways to look at horses. To some of us the living horse is a work of art. Even the structure of the skeleton, the bones, as depicted by George Stubbs in his *Anatomy of the Horse*, give us a fair comprehension of the easy motion, the force of propulsion rising into speed, the interaction and integration of many separate and sometimes minute parts which comprise the horse in action. The plough horse straining at the traces with powerful stride and deliberate rhythm, the Hackney trotting with

George Stubbs, ARA (1724–1806): *Pumpkin with a Stable-lad*, 1774

Pumpkin was painted as a five-year-old, having been foaled in 1769, sired by Matchem out of Old Squirt. The joint owners of the horse were Charles James Fox and the Hon. Thomas Foley.

light step and alert head, the polo pony jinking and swerving like an athlete, the hunter or 'chaser gliding easily over a great fence, the Thoroughbred with his ears pricked, galloping gracefully down to the starting stalls, all form pictures in our minds which have much the same attributes as fine paintings or drawings.

And as though these graceful and powerful movements were not enough, one can also enjoy those motionless attitudes of heads and ears and eyes – heads high, ears pricked forward or pressed back in exertion or in anger, eyes gazing deep into the distance like those of the winning colt in that wonderful story *The Look of Eagles*. We are warmed by the range of their colours, the sheen of their coats in the sunlight, the ripple of muscles and ligaments. There is a poetry in all of this, such as 'Banjo' Patterson, that great Australian poet, describes in his *Rio Grande*:

> The champions of the days long fled,
> They moved around with noiseless tread –
> Bay, chestnut, brown and black.

And I can remember, one day at the races, a ghostly grey suddenly rushing up through a field of tiring horses, fighting it out to the finish and winning like a flash of silver. These are the aesthetics of the horse, whether in life or in art.

There are many who look at horses anthropomorphically, who see in them likenesses to humans: human feelings, thoughts, ambitions, sorrows – all attributes of our own psychology. I have sometimes made myself unpopular by pointing out the very limited *intelligence* horses really have. They are creatures of habit and discipline, and are taught very little by example or kindness and almost everything by gentle force and the patient denial of their instincts and whims. Horses have no sense of humour although, like all animals, they play. But have you ever seen a horse smile, like a dog smiles? Or have you seen one wag his tail?!

This is not to disparage the horse, or to deny him recognition of his inherent fine qualities. What horses tend to remind us of, perhaps deep in our own unconscious, is the instinctual life which flows forever below the layers of restraint laid down by the millenia of civilization. We humans have our own hidden aggressions, avarice, competitiveness in one form or another, which we hope are well controlled. We also have reserves of energy, stamina, courage which we see reflected in the actions of horses in situations of stress – the all-out finish of a race, the clearing of a high obstacle, or the plough or draught horse moving an almost immovable object. In a different way we can see a mare nursing, disciplining and protecting her foal, just as a woman who is a mother does with her child. But these are instinctual things, not products of intellect or of civilization.

And so we project our own psyches into our observations of horses, seeing in them such desirable attributes as courage, loyalty, love, ambition. Such things are learned, on the whole, by man. What we see in a horse as courage is an instinctive will to win. And so we also project our own aggressions and jealousies into our thoughts about him, praising his will to win or damning him when he sulks or shows timidity, judging him all the while on a human scale. It is perhaps *good* that we do this to a certain extent, and I admit I am prone to the same illusions. But I have so often seen these illusions degenerate into cloying sentimentality (as seen in many of Landseer's paintings) which can be as foolish as it is unreal. It reminds me of baby-talk among grown-ups. Let us look at the horse as he *is*, a vital being in his own right, with his own aura of beauty, a noble work of art by that greatest of artists, Nature.

It is a sad fact that British sporting art has been looked down on by critics and the intelligentsia from the eighteenth century to the present day. It is of course true that many horse pictures of the eighteenth and nineteenth centuries were stilted and unimaginative. (There have always been bad artists in any century and in any genre.) But the best so-called sporting artists have always been able to hold their own technically and aesthetically with the best landscapists and portraitists of their day. If one tries to forget the social or sporting significance of the vast number of these paintings of horse racing, horses jumping, horses standing proudly with their smug owners and trainers and grooms, and looks rather at the finer examples of horse portraiture such as those produced by Stubbs and Ben Marshall, one is faced with an entirely different experience. Through these finer artists we realize that the horse is as noble and graceful a vehicle for heightening our visual senses, for producing that subtlety of emotion created by line and form and colour as we tend to find in the skilful artistic depiction of other objects such as people, houses, trees, fields, gardens or ships.

In fact, it isn't really difficult to look at a horse portrait as one would at an abstract painting (say, a Ben Nicholson): forget the *uses* of the horse, the connotation of sport or speed, and you can understand that his real beauty, his impact as an aesthetic object lies in his lines, the fluidity of his form, the suggestion of life and vitality created by the drawing and brushwork of the artist. Leaf through this book and you will see countless examples in which, if you will suppress your own memories of horses, you can enjoy the pure imagery of their attitudes, shapes and colours.

It is often written that Stubbs himself resented the economic necessity of painting horse portraits for rich clients. I wonder. I think he saw in the horse, in his alertness and muscularity, a way of representing life itself in all its movement, form, vitality, colour, strife and mystery. His horses are alive and beautiful because they were in his soul; he saw them as symbols of many life forces rather than as mere conveyances, necessities, implements. Just as his paintings of lions, tigers, zebras, cheetahs and other wild animals glow with vibrant power, so his horses give off an aura of grace, transforming the perils of energy and wildness into a controlled sense of tense expectation. In addition to his use of the horse as an object of pleasure and delight, we can also see in his backgrounds a reverential feeling for landscape. He uses landscape as a quiet foil against which to bring out more clearly these forces of life and power.

But, like all things in life, those which we enjoy the most are most closely related to our own feelings and experiences. Here in this book the horse lover, of whatever avocation or profession, will find many delights for the eye as well as the pleasures of remembrance of equine friends of the past. It all adds up to the fact that there have always been horses in my heart. For the same reason, because they are beautiful and graceful animals, I believe that the horse is an archetypal symbol which will always stir up deep and moving ancestral memories in every human being.

PAUL MELLON

LEFT The White Horse near Uffington, Berkshire,
England, 1st century AD
RIGHT Bronze model of a Scythian archer or possibly
an Amazon, Etruscan, c. 500 BC

The hill figures of England and Scotland, made by cutting
away turf to expose chalk deposits, are of unknown origin
and are unique to the British Isles. Like the chalk hill figure,
the Scythian archer exhibits a primitive feeling for movement,
unsupported by any understanding of form or anatomy.

LEFT Detail of a chariot race from a Greek vase, 490–80 BC
RIGHT James Seymour (1702–52): detail of *The Chaise
Match run on Newmarket Heath on Wednesday, 29 August 1750*

Chariot racing was a popular sport in the Greek and Roman
worlds, and contests continued well into the Middle Ages.
Seymour's painting portrays an eighteenth-century revival that
was characteristic of the eccentric habits of wealthy sportsmen
at the time. The scene records a wager between the third Earl of
March and the first Earl of Eglinton on the one part, and
Colonel Theobald O'Taafe and Andrew Sproule on the other,
for 10,000 guineas that a four-wheeled carriage drawn by four
horses and carrying one man could travel nineteen miles in one
hour. The wager was won by the two Earls with a little over
six minutes to spare.

Signal.

LEFT David Dalby of York
(1790–1840): *Signal, a Grey Arab,
with a Groom in the Desert*, 1829
RIGHT *Grooming a Stallion*,
Persian miniature, late 16th century

There was a vogue which started
in the time of John Wootton
(1683?–1764) but which flourished
in the nineteenth century, for
painting Arab horses against a desert
background. The composition was
usually suitably embellished with a
turbaned and robed groom, and
perhaps a tent or palm tree in the
background. It was a romantic
conception for normally neither
owners, artists nor horses had ever
seen the deserts of Arabia.

In the miniature from a Persian
book of verse the artist's portrayal of
a similar subject is far more practical.
Although the groom has yet to
remove a certain amount of rugs and
surcingles before he can effectively
groom his horse, he has sensibly tied
two of its legs together so that he will
not be kicked while doing so. The
inscription on the painting reads
'said to be an Arab'. Arab horses
were highly prized in Persia as they
were in the Western world.

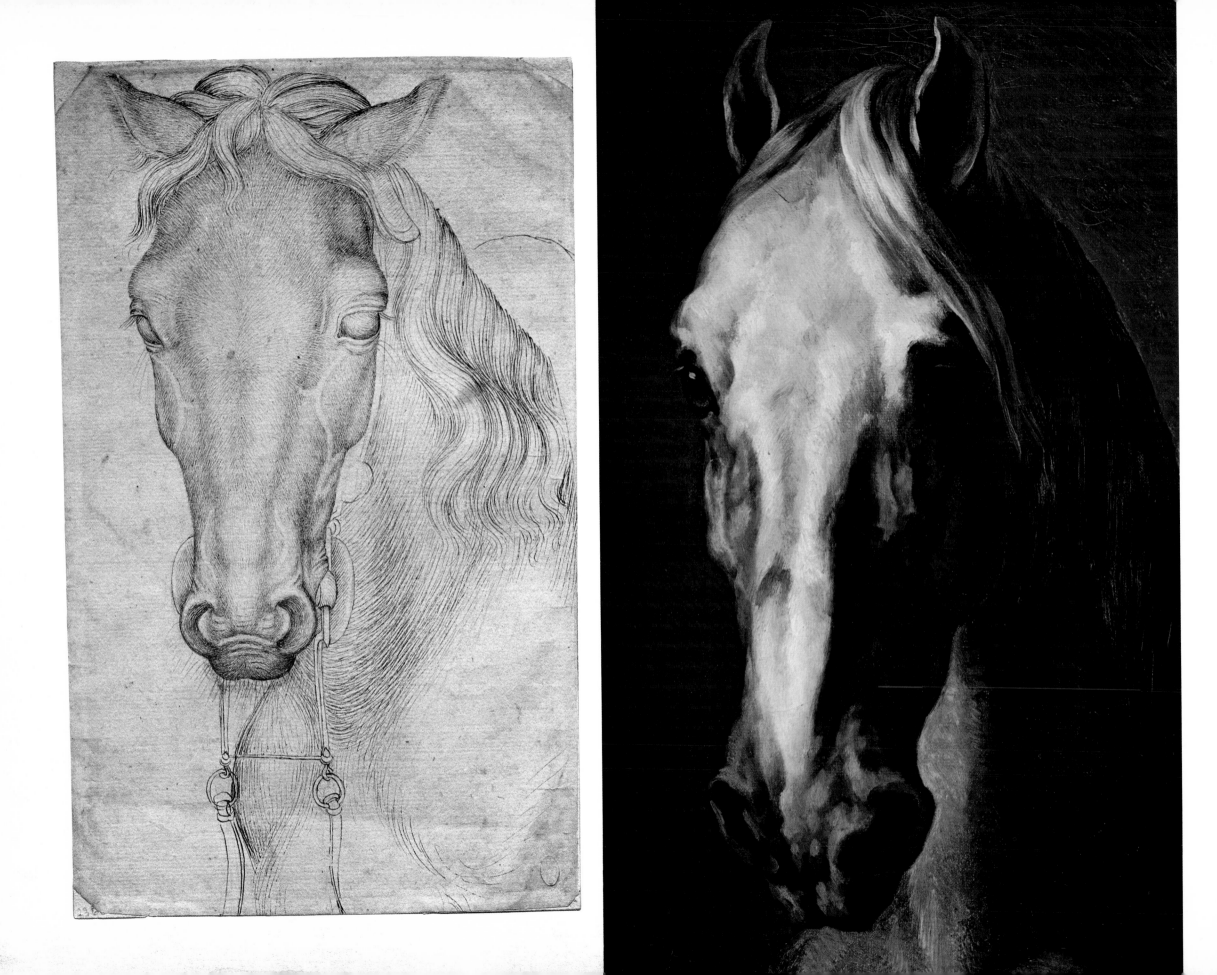

FAR LEFT Antonio Pisanello (1395–1455): *Study of the Neck and Head of a bridled Horse seen face on*, c. 1430–40
LEFT Théodore Géricault (1791–1824): *Head of a White Horse*, 1810–12
RIGHT George Stubbs: Two studies for *The Anatomy of the Horse*, 1758–9

Separated in date of execution by some four centuries, the two heads on the left appear superficially to be remarkably similar, but closer inspection reveals the differences that have occurred through selective breeding, away from the heavy war horse and ceremonial horse towards the race horse and carriage horse.

The two drawings by Stubbs show differing stages in the dissection of the horse. His great work of dissection and drawing, resulting in the publication of *The Anatomy of the Horse* in 1766, enabled him to unite scientific accuracy and artistic genius in his portrayals of the horse.

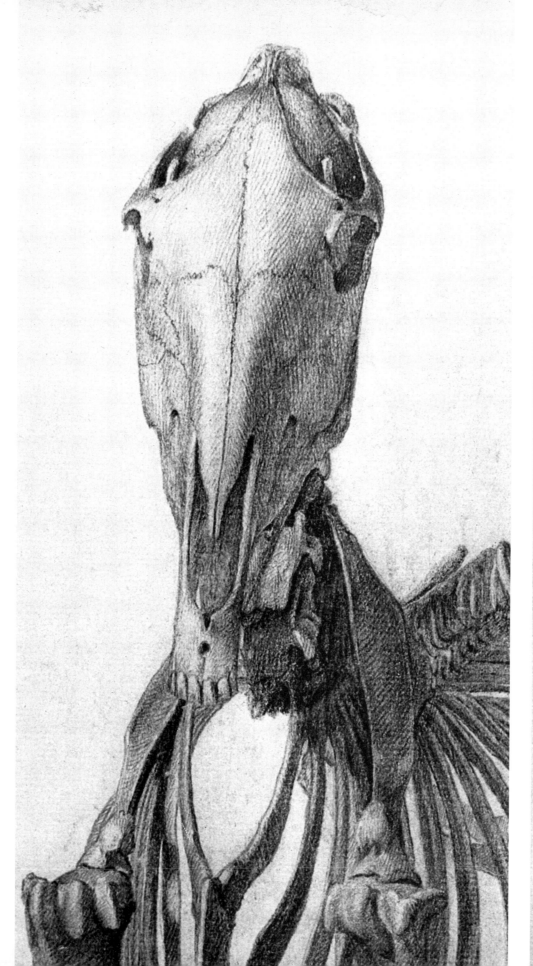

ABOVE Benjamin Herring (d. 1871): *The Start of the Race for the Cambridgeshire Stakes, Newmarket, Tuesday, 22 October 1867*
RIGHT Edouard Manet (1832–1883): *The Races at Longchamp, 1864*

Both pictures, painted within three years of one another, share the fact that they are imaginary views seen from a totally impractical standpoint.

INTRODUCTION

From first contacts as children we quickly come to realize that horses can be alarmingly fast in their reactions, quick to bite and kick, and inclined to run off if anything untoward happens. How did the horse evolve? How did it come to be tamed – if that is the right expression for a creature with such an equivocal relationship with man? What is the connection with strength and power that inspires man to produce works of art identifying his feeling for the horse, and how has man's life been enriched by the association?

The practical advantages from mastery over the horse have been fairly obvious. The pack horse, war horse, carriage horse and the hack all performed useful functions until the development of the internal combustion engine. There is, on the other hand, an aspect of the animal that has appealed to the more sophisticated requirements of human nature – the need for excitement, for aesthetic satisfaction and as an expression of spiritual aspiration. To be seated on horseback, five feet above contradiction, brings a man authority; to gallop hell-for-leather with the wind in his face lends the rider wings, as if he were at one with the gods. All these facets have from very early times appealed to the creative and artistic side of man, resulting in artifacts, sculpture, prints, drawings and paintings into which it is the purpose of the succeeding pages to give some small insight.

The civilizations in whose cultures the horse featured, and through whose art the images have come down to us, are numerous and they reflect the migration and development of the animal through many centuries. Stone Age, Scythian, Assyrian, Persian, Chinese, Indian, Greek and Roman, Medieval, Renaissance and Western European: each name conjures up visions of nomadic tribes, of primitive hunters, sophisticated but cruel warriors, aesthetes or eager sportsmen. It is largely through their art that we know them.

The natural history, development and migration of the horse have been expertly dealt with elsewhere, and this short essay only warrants a brief summary in an attempt to indicate how the different types of horse arrived in those locations from where we have artistic evidence of their

LEFT Cave painting from Lascaux, France, c. 10,000 BC

RIGHT ABOVE Gold belt plaque, Sakic culture, 4th century BC
RIGHT BELOW Detail of the Great Vessel from the Tomb of the Princess at Vix, Greek-Italian origin, 5th century BC

presence. Two great migrations occurred from North America before the Ice Age. One moved down through the isthmus to form herds in South America, which later became extinct (hence the great advantage enjoyed by the *Conquistadores* when they arrived so many centuries later mounted on horseback, the natives thinking they were monsters capable of dividing themselves into two parts). The other great migration moved east across the Bering Strait – then but an adjoining stretch of land – into the Kolyma Plain, to Eastern Siberia and so across the vast plains of the Steppes, south-eastward into China, westward and southward into the Near and Middle East, and into the heavy forests of Europe. The evidence of these movements has chiefly been discovered through fossil findings, but vestiges of the wild horse still exist today. At the end of the nineteenth century the explorer Colonel Przewalski presented a specimen of a horse, which had been found by hunters in the Gobi Desert, to the Zoological Museum in St Petersburg; it proved to be the type of wild horse extant since prehistoric times, and long thought to be extinct. These horses may still exist in small numbers in the wild, but their survival appears to depend on the examples kept in zoos. Another lighter type, the Tarpan, lived up to the mid-nineteenth century, when it was exterminated because it was damaging crops in the Ukraine. Other breeds undoubtedly evolved and died out and cross-strains must have appeared as these different types interbred. A heavier breed appears on the Stone Age wall paintings in southern France (*c.* 10,000 BC) but it would probably be unwise to interpret these lively images as accurate portrayals, for the pictures are thought to have some religious significance. Thus, according to whether or not they could adapt to their environment, some species of horse became extinct; others survived.

There is no way of knowing when man was first able to take horses into captivity and to domesticate them, but the process appears to have taken place in the Steppes, those vast plains to the north of the mountain ranges stretching from the Black Sea to Manchuria and the Pacific, inhabited by aggressive nomadic tribes, the Scythians, Huns, Turks, Tartars and Mongols. Among earliest evidence of domesticated horses are rather sophisticated snaffle bits from Asia Minor dating from the late Bronze Age, about the fifteenth and fourteenth centuries BC. These metal bits came to replace those made from bones and deer horn, although the latter may have continued to be used on chariot horses: the chariots themselves appeared during the first millennium BC. So we have evidence of domesticated horses going back some 3,500 years, although the use of the pack horse as a swifter form of transport than oxen, and one needing less water, probably predates the bitted horse by many centuries.

Two works of art illustrate that the types of harness and accoutrement in use in the fifth and fourth centuries BC were common to eastern Siberia and the Mediterranean. The Hermitage in Leningrad contains a group of treasures gathered from provincial centres in the early eighteenth century by Peter the Great. Among them is an exquisite fourth-century-BC rendering of tamed horses in cast gold in the form of a belt plaque. This ornament, probably deriving from the Sakic tribes of Kazakhstan, west of Mongolia, depicts two men and a woman beneath a tree holding two saddled and bridled horses. The plaque has about it a breathless time-spanning quality. Taki horses (as the Mongolians called the Przewalski horse), with hogged manes, stand grazing on the left of the plaque, wearing modern-looking bridles furnished with double nose bands, brow bands, cheek straps and throat lashes. They appear to be bitless and are held by a cord secured to the lower jaw. The saddles are held on with a surcingle, and their long tails are plaited. It is astonishing that such equipment should have changed so little in some 2,400 years. The horsemen represented here were from the Steppes. They were nomads who seldom lived a settled life by raising crops; rather they ate horses and pickled horse flesh, drank curdled horse milk, and buried their leaders surrounded by their horses, which had been slaughtered when they died. These Huns, Mongols and Tartars, whose lively and imaginative art was preserved by their icy tombs, were the scourge of the civilizations of China, the Near East and the West up to the time of Genghis Khan in the thirteenth century, when they controlled China and had overrun Persia and Mesopotamia.

The Museum at Châtillon-sur-Seine near Dijon contains the treasures from the tomb site at the nearby village of Vix which, well preserved by river silt, were excavated after the Second World War. The discoveries included a Greek wine mixer, a work of art of astonishing quality and the largest preserved from antiquity, cast in bronze, of South Italian origin and dating from the fifth century BC. It must have been shipped north by wine merchants as a tribute to an influential Celtic ruler. The neck of the Great Vessel is decorated with a frieze which shows a procession including eight horse-drawn four-wheeled chariots. The bridles on the horses bear very close resemblance to those on the horses from the eastern Steppes.

The two factors which regulate offensive action in time of war are weaponry and mobility. Chariots, synonymous with the power of Greece and Rome, had been standard military vehicles from very early times in the Near East. They enjoyed a manoeuvrability on their own terrain which was only really shared by tanks in the Middle East during the Second World War. The Sumerians used solid-wheeled battle chariots drawn by Onagers, or wild asses. These were employed virtually as battering rams to break the front line of the enemy's foot soldiers, but subsequent refinements such as spoke wheels and light basketwork-bodied chariots drawn by horses and carrying a driver with a goad, and perhaps an archer standing next to him, rendered the vehicle much more versatile. Scythe-bearing chariots were first used by the Persians at the battle of Arbela in 331 BC.

One of the earliest artistic representations of horse-drawn chariots features in the public state rooms of the Assyrian palace at Nineveh on the banks of the Tigris, where there were seventh-century-BC large stone wall-slabs carved in bas-relief showing the victories enjoyed in war by the ruthless Assyrians over their neighbouring enemies. Visiting emissaries being received at the palace would have had a chance to see, represented in sculpture, the tethered prisoners, severed heads and arrow-stricken corpses of those who had had the temerity to resist Assyrian power. The stone carvings, some of which are now in the British Museum, illustrate among their anecdotal propaganda the chariots and horses of the Assyrians' brutal armies. Horses at that time were too small in build and too light to carry warriors, who would anyway have considered themselves to look ridiculous appearing in the battlefield astride such little animals.

The small horses and chariots gradually came to be relegated to funeral games, processions and races. The pagan symbols of the games, which governed the rules of the chariot races, were founded on an equation between the pattern of men's lives and that of Nature. Hence the eggs displayed showed the competitors the number of laps they had completed, representing the cycles of the sun and moon and rebirth. With the passing of time, these rules came to be observed more in the letter than in the spirit. In the latter days of the Roman Empire chariot racing became a sport which created even greater excitement and violence than football today. The limited contests, when rulers proved their prowess, changed by degrees into public spectacles, held in vast arenas like the Circus Maximus in Rome or the Hippodrome in Constantinople. Professional charioteers became swaggering public heroes, their deeds commemorated in the decorations on wine vessels and mosaics. Involvement of politicians and the partisanship of the masses frequently resulted in public disturbances and rioting in which sometimes thousands of people were killed. Finally, the sport fell into disrepute, although contests continued well into the Middle Ages.

During the first millennium BC progressively larger horses were bred in the Near East, and they and camels appeared on the battlefields as the prototype of modern cavalry. Assyrian expansion, which started toward the close of the Bronze Age (c. 1200 BC), reached its height between 911 and 612 BC, eventually falling to the Medians and Chaldeans. Much wider conquests in the Near East were achieved with the rise of the Persian Empire (c. 550–486 BC). The Persian king Darius, who came to power in 521 BC, extended his kingdom from Macedonia to the Indus.

The horses of the ancient Persian Empire are illustrated in bas-relief carvings on the stairways of the Apadana at Persepolis. The royal riding horses are about fifteen to twenty per cent larger than the royal chariot

horses. The former are of the ancient Nicaean type, thought to have originated with the cross-breeding of central Asiatic and African horses, and to be the ancestors of the Persian Arab. Horses from different parts of the Empire are shown in the procession and include Scythian, Sogdian (Turkestan), Skudrian (Greece), Lydian (Turkey) and Libyan breeds. With the royal horses, these fall into three distinct types, but because of artistic and possibly even religious conventions, one cannot identify them with any certainty.

In 334 BC the youthful Alexander the Great crossed the Hellespont with infantry, covered by the then enormous force of five thousand Macedonian cavalry. A superb tactician, he deployed his horsemen with deadly effect and conquered all the Persian Empire. The use of cavalry in battle had reached its full potential relatively rapidly and the period between the seventh and fourth centuries BC saw a marked development of the horse in the Near East. If we compare the horses in the Assyrian and Persian wall decorations with the stone carvings from the Parthenon it becomes clear that, if still small, the horses had become much finer in conformation.

During the Classical Greek era art achieved a hitherto unknown perfection; a style emulated by the Romans and indeed forming the basis of Western art from the period of the re-discovery of Classical learning and art at the Renaissance. The frieze from the interior of the colonnade of the Parthenon is among the best-known classical sculpture from the Golden Age, commonplace, if at all, only in the eye of the beholder. Created under the direction of the famous sculptor Phidias, it represents, according to the traditional view, the Panathenaic procession celebrating the birthday of the goddess Athene, although the theory has recently been advanced that it commemorates the heroes of Marathon. The work, carried out in the middle of the fifth century BC, displays a realism and vitality, together with a three-dimensional quality, which are very forceful. The detailed attention to muscles and veins and to producing an alertness of gesture and movement testifies to Phidias's close study of horses.

Another striking horse sculpture dating from *c.* 350 BC is featured on

LEFT Detail from the west frieze of the interior colonnade of the Parthenon, Greek, 5th century BC

RIGHT Head and forepart of one of the four horses which formed part of the chariot group surmounting the Mausoleum at Halicarnassus, Greek, *c.* 350 BC

the tomb of King Mausolus at Halicarnassus on the coast of Asia Minor. The Mausoleum, known as one of the Seven Wonders of the World, was shattered by an earthquake in the Middle Ages, and later plundered by the Knights of Malta for repairs to their nearby castle, but among the remains is the over-lifesize forepart of a horse, with remnants of its bridle, which at one time formed part of the four-horse chariot described by Pliny as surmounting this enormous tomb. The symbolic meaning was presumably that the spirit of the king would be driven by the horses and drawn by the chariot into the after-life.

Well-bred horses arrived later in China, after they had become rooted in the Near East and the eastern Mediterranean. Contact with the West was established in due course through the Silk Route of Samarkand; to the north, the sandy wastes of the Gobi Desert were the barrier which most prevented contact between the Chinese and their horse-borne Hunnish nomadic northern neighbours. The Chinese were concerned to keep these marauding barbaric tribes at bay, and with this objective in mind they constructed the Great Wall. During the Han Dynasty (206 BC–AD 222) an embassy despatched by the Emperor Wu to entreat with dissident tribesmen occupying Turkestan learnt of the Western civilizations of Thrace and Macedonia. They brought back reports of horses, much larger and more impressive than the Mongolian ponies, which had formerly been the only breed the Chinese had known. Wu mounted two armed expeditions against Ta Yüan (now in Russian Turkestan) with a view to bringing back some of these renowned horses for breeding purposes. After rigorous campaigns the second force succeeded, and the new breed was commemorated in memorable works of art, including the celebrated figure of *The Flying Horse standing on one leg on a Swallow* (Eastern Han, AD 25–222). These horses, although doubtless stylized by the artists, nevertheless reveal a distinct conformation with their broad chests and dished faces. Later the T'ang Dynasty, which spanned nearly three centuries (AD 618–907), saw the creation of some of the finest Chinese horse figures. These models, with others of attendants, etc., were placed in burial tombs and, as elsewhere in early civilizations, were intended to accompany the deceased on his travels after death.

In the West during the Dark Ages the Western Roman Empire had fallen in the fifth century at the hands of the Barbarians – the Visigoths, Huns, Vandals and Ostrogoths – from the north and north east. It had seen the sudden growth of Islam in the seventh century when, in less than a hundred years, scattered Arabic tribes had united to establish a powerful empire stretching from the Near East along the south side of the Mediterranean to Spain. It had witnessed, too, the empire of Charlemagne in the eighth century, when this champion of Christendom united Western Europe, and the rule of Byzantium in the ninth and tenth centuries over modern Turkey and Greece with footholds in Sicily and Southern Italy.

The triumph of Christianity after the chaos following the fall of Roman power produced an archetype, a horseman who tempered soldierliness with piety, strength with courtesy and gallantry with devotion. This was the soldier of Christ, the mounted knight who followed the code of chivalry (Old French *Chevalerie*, from *cheval*: horse). The ideal is perhaps best represented in Albrecht Dürer's (1471–1528) engraving of 1513, *The Knight, Death and the Devil*. The armour-clad knight sits astride his mount walking past a small medieval hill town. Death, wearing a snake-entwined crown, laconically shows him his hour-glass while the Devil, portrayed as a hideous beast, plods behind him. The Knight, however, with visor raised, does not look around but keeps his gaze fixed ahead of him, a pilgrim in God's service. The reality, on the other hand, was probably to be more closely identified with Dürer's *Soldier on Horseback with a Lance* (p. 69) in the Albertina, Vienna. This watercoloured drawing bears the inscription, '*Dz ist die Rustung zw der Zeit in Tewtzschland gewest*' ('This is the armour worn at the time in Germany'). Similarly portrayed, yet with a subtle change of emphasis, both horse and rider have lost their idealistic stance. Altogether more convincing as a realistic image, this horseman, with his emaciated, hard-bitten appearance, seems to represent the type of mounted warrior

LEFT *The Flying Horse standing on one leg on a Swallow*, Chinese, Eastern Han Dynasty, AD 25–222

RIGHT Albrecht Dürer (1471–1528): *The Knight, Death and the Devil*, 1513
BELOW Detail of *The Triumph of an Emperor* (possibly Anastasius I), known as *The Barberini Ivory*, Constantinople, *c.* AD 500

who took part in the Crusades, who pushed the Turks back when they had nearly reached the gates of Vienna and who expelled the Moors from Spain. This is not to say that these soldiers did not spend much of their time fighting one another in support of their local quarrelling overlords. In fact, it was partly with a view to channelling this exuberant aggressiveness away from the home countries that the idea occurred of carrying war to the infidel, and bringing Jerusalem back into Christian hands.

With the emergence of the Middle Ages, Christendom was firmly established in Western Europe as a coherent hierarchical social structure, capable of defending itself against infidel and barbarian, and enabling a stability which encouraged the growth of centres of learning and of the arts. Human endeavour was consecrated towards the worship of God and expressed itself mainly through the media of architecture and sculpture. Such art confined itself almost exclusively to religious themes and there was little scope for the artists to engage in making images of horses. A few subjects such as *St Martin and the Beggar, St George and the Dragon* and *The Conversion of St Paul* lent themselves to the inclusion of horses in the composition, but the predominance of Church patronage acted as a restrictive factor in the appearance of horses in religious art right down through the seventeenth century.

A breakthrough occurred in the second half of the fifteenth century when, at the time of the Reformation, engravings and woodcuts became established, particularly in Northern Europe, as a popular form of art. Although the subject-matter was primarily religious, a much stronger secular element crept in, and in the prints of Austrian, German, Swiss, Flemish and Netherlandish masters, we can see the artists indulging themselves in scenes of fantasy or from contemporary life. Woodcut and engraved prints were made and reproduced to commemorate the equestrian feats of the ruling classes. Riders spared little expense in obtaining for themselves magnificent suits of armour, with feathers in their helmets and gaily painted shields. The horses too were scarcely less well decked out and the rules and practice of jousting developed to a point of expertise comparable with chariot racing earlier, and later with nineteenth-century hunting. Unlike chariot racing, jousting really remained an aristocratic pastime, but a living could with difficulty be made by professional performers. Kings and their courtiers entered the lists to demonstrate their manliness and to impress their ladies. There was a fashion in the early sixteenth century under the patronage of such figures as the Emperor Maximilian I to commission rather grandiose triumphal arches and processions executed on individual blocks or in a series of woodcuts by the leading German masters of the day. Dürer, Burgkmair and Lucas Cranach, among others, produced highly ornate processional and jousting scenes in which the cutting was executed with inordinate skill to show elaborate suits of armour, plumed helmets and armoured horses with flowing manes and tails. Although jousting was effectively no longer practised much beyond the sixteenth century, its romantic pull was evident in the Eglinton Tournament of 1839, a contest held at enormous expense in heavy rain at Eglinton Castle. The 'knights' were so unpractised in the art that some had problems with rusting armour.

Throughout the Middle Ages the romantic concept was directed towards heavy cavalry – knights in full armour on heavy horses. The weakness of the heavy war horse was revealed, as every schoolboy knows, on the field of Agincourt (1415), when the ponderous French heavy cavalry were struck down by the arrows of the English long-bowmen. Heavy horses gradually became more and more redundant in war and by the outbreak of the English Civil War they were effectively finished. Sir Arthur Haselrig's plate-armoured cavalry, raised for Parliament and referred to as 'Haselrig's Lobsters', did not acquit themselves well in the field. Heavy cavalry, however, were retained throughout the Thirty Years' War. Dragoons were a cumbrous musket-bearing adaptation current in England in the eighteenth century, while Europe concentrated on developing the light-horse mobile Hussar. The Crimean campaign must have seen one of the last active appearances of the Heavy Brigade, for by then cavalry had been transformed by Frederick the Great and his cavalry general Seidlitz. In eighteenth-century England the Earl of Pembroke was prominent in

promoting change. The clumsy, badly forged cavalry swords gave way to well-balanced sharp sabres and the accent in a charge was placed on dash and speed, a technique for which the fox-hunting enthusiasts among the cavalry officers had a special aptitude. While this change swept over Protestant Europe, the French who had always had a penchant for heavier horses and for the *manège* as a more disciplined and aristocratic form of horsemanship, tended towards a more conservative approach. The Duke of Wellington praised the French horse as more manageable than his own, but there was no doubt about the effectiveness of a headlong charge by light cavalry when it was properly directed.

It is commonly thought, and probably correctly, that the Crusades (1096–1291) brought the West into contact with Arab horses. It seems unlikely, at the time of the sudden expansion of Islam in the seventh century, that Arab horses would have been transported across the desert to the Barbary Coast and then into southern Spain; the invaders would have taken the North African Barbs with them and there is evidence of a native Andalusian horse. However, Arab horses could well have found their way into Italy via the Crusader staging posts of Cyprus, Malta and Sicily. Sicily was under Muslim control by the eighth century, later to be recaptured by Norman mercenaries in the pay of the Pope, but by then the Arab stock was already established there. The Gonzaga family of Mantua bred horses of oriental as well as domestic ancestry. The paintings of the School of Giulio Romano in the Palazzo del Té at Mantua illustrate the quality of the horses in the Gonzaga stables.

In 1514 Francesco Gonzaga sold some horses to Henry VIII of England. Henry was anxious to build up the Royal Stud at Eltham, and acquired horses not only from the Gonzagas but also from Ferdinand of Aragon and from the Emperor Charles V. The stables at Eltham, which had been in existence for some time before Henry's reign, continued in operation, although badly run, until the seventeenth century, when their destruction was ordered by Oliver Cromwell during the period of the Commonwealth. Henry VIII also kept a racing establishment at Greenwich. The latter concern was maintained by Queen Elizabeth I, who founded another Royal Stud at Tutbury in Staffordshire. The Tutbury Stud received the best horses, mostly likely descendants of those imported by her father. The movement was not one-sided, and Italy imported horses from England. Racing was common in the towns of Northern Italy, and Siena had its own stud. By the fifteenth century the *Palio* was a popular race. It was preceded by a long and spectacular procession of all the competing *contrade* (districts). By the sixteenth century boys, wearing the liveries of their teams and riding bareback, galloped over the sand-covered stones three times round the Piazza. Needless to say, many fell off and there was frequent cheating. In some respects this race, which is still run today, has something of the flavour of the old chariot races, and the Catholic Church, perhaps recalling the pagan aspects of the old chariot competitions, allows the horses to be actually taken into the churches for a light-hearted blessing before the commencement of the race.

The flowering of art, which manifested itself first in Italy in the fourteenth and fifteenth centuries and which later spread through Western Europe, witnessed new approaches both spiritual and theoretical. It has broadly been said that the Renaissance occurred concurrently with a degeneration of Christian values; that the mystical qualities of Giotto were superseded by the self-glorification of Man, created in the image of God, as seen in the High Renaissance masters. What is certain is that the strict iconography of the Middle Ages was broken down to give artists a much wider range of subject-matter and that, among other objects, they were able once more to give their attention to horses in art.

As far as precedent went, they had very little to go on. The excavations of the eighteenth and nineteenth centuries had not yet revealed those bronze horses of antiquity which then still lay under silt and lava. The most famous of the unburied statues was the *Equestrian Statue of Marcus Aurelius*, which had stood throughout the Middle Ages on a site near St John Lateran in Rome. It was moved to its present position in front of the Capitol in 1538 under Michelangelo's supervision. The statues of

Equestrian Statue of Marcus Aurelius, Roman, 2nd century AD

Ancient Rome, once so plentiful, had suffered at the hands of early Christian iconoclasts. The barbarians from the north were also responsible for wanton destruction and for melting down bronzes in order to use the metal. The *Equestrian Statue of Marcus Aurelius*, however, survived probably because of a continuing belief that this bronze of the Roman philosopher-Emperor represented the first Christtian Emperor, Constantine the Great (AD 306–37). It is perhaps unfortunate that this rather sober survival from ancient sculpture should have had such an influence on equestrian statuary from the Middle Ages throughout the fifteenth century right up until the time of Pollaiuolo and Leonardo, who looked at the horse afresh from life and from antique friezes. Apart from isolated examples, like the statue at Bamberg and the equestrian portrait of Charlemagne at Aix-la-Chapelle, it was the fifteenth century which saw the re-introduction of life-size bronze equestrian statuary. Wooden models had been made, but these proved not to be lasting. In 1436 a fresco was commissioned from Paolo Uccello (1396/7–1475): an equestrian portrait of the English *condottiere* and rogue Sir John Hawkwood (p. 64). He is seen mounted, his horse standing on a painted sarcophagus, in the Duomo in Florence. Within twenty years the first bronze equestrian monument of Erasmo da Narni or Gattamelata (The Tiger Cat), Captain General of the Republic of Venice, by Donatello (c. 1386–1466), was completed and set up in the Piazza del Santo in Padua (p. 66). Then, thirty years later, Verrocchio (1436–88) made the monument in Venice to Bartolommeo Colleoni, the military general. Despite striking differences of approach to the sitters, all three of these great Renaissance masters have treated the horses almost identically. Each was conversant with the Aurelian prototype in Rome, and also with the classical bronze horses above the entrance to St Mark's in Venice.

From the drawings of Pisanello (1395–1455) in the Louvre and those of Leonardo (1452–1519) at Windsor Castle, we can see that Renaissance artists took as deep an interest in horses as in the human form. It is odd, however, that the early examples of Renaissance equestrian wall painting and sculpture should have relied so heavily on two antique prototypes rather than the livelier and more imaginative interpretations which Antonio Pollaiuolo (1433–98) and Leonardo discovered in the rearing horses from friezes on classical sarcophagi. Technically, of course, a large bronze statue of a rearing horse presented special problems, and Pollaiuolo's and Leonardo's schemes never materialized in sculpture, although drawn studies survive. Both artists made studies for an equestrian monument to Francesco Sforza, Duke of Milan, and Leonardo made further studies for a statue of the Milanese commander Trivulzio (p. 66–7). Leonardo drew the Duke of Milan's horses from life in their stables. He made measurements, and the sketches in his notebooks at Windsor Castle reveal the probing interest of the scientist-artist; a quality which produced work of a similarly inquiring vein some three hundred years later by George Stubbs.

A form of sculpture which became popular in Italy during the Renaissance was the bronze statuette. Like the full-size statue it was a revival from classical art, but its intimate scale rendered it suitable for the private collector and as a present. Among the most talented, as far as the production of little equestrian monuments were concerned, were Andrea Riccio (c. 1470–1532), a native of Padua, and Giambologna (1529–1608), a Flemish sculptor who worked in Italy.

Paolo Uccello, with Pisanello, was first in the field of horse painting in the Renaissance. His panels depicting the battle of San Romano, painted to decorate the ground-floor hall of the Medici Palace, are now dispersed in Florence, Paris and London (p. 65). The battle Uccello commemorated, a minor engagement between Florentines and Sienese, was fought within about fifty years of the battle of Agincourt and used similar heavy cavalry. The artist evidently took liberties, adapting the scene to look more like a tournament, and the paintings were even laughingly referred to in his own day as 'the tilting match'. However, the spade-bits and spurs were doubtless accurate enough, and the heavy horses, like the early chariots, were probably employed as battering rams when their riders were not engaged in hand-to-hand combat.

Uccello was a very unorthodox and eccentric artist, in many respects unique. His vision at once looked back to the Middle Ages and forward

Paolo Uccello (1396/7–1475): *The Hunt,* after 1460

31

to modern art. His work sometimes contained an almost cubist quality, unknown, except in the drawings of the seventeenth-century Genoese artist Luca Cambiaso, until the present century, and at the same time it offers an inexplicable mystery and timelessness. He was one of those painters, who appear from time to time in the annals of art, who loved portraying animals; others who may be included are Albrecht Dürer, Stefano della Bella, Johann Ridinger, Jean-Baptiste Oudry, George Stubbs and Edwin Landseer.

Uccello was an originator. The concept of the flat images of the Norman horsemen on *The Bayeux Tapestry*, and of the little detailed enamel-coloured drawings on the pages of medieval manuscripts, was gone at a stroke by his declaration that in future painting was to be three-dimensional, aided by perspective and lighting. His painting *The Hunt*, in the Ashmolean Museum, Oxford, depicts animals and men running along carefully calculated invisible lines of perspective into a dark Gothic forest. *The Battle of San Romano* also reveals this obsession with perspective. A fallen soldier lies straight, obediently pointing out a perspective line, while his mounted companions manoeuvre their lances to support the artist's mathematically calculated composition.

Perspective was later developed in a classical manner by Raphael in his *Lo Sposalizio* and reached its wilder shores in mannerist painting. The effect was to enable the spectator to see into a flat panel or canvas, and for the objects portrayed on it to acquire what Bernard Berenson described as 'tactile values'. This illusion was reinforced by judicious lighting effects, and in Uccello's *San Romano* paintings the artificial lighting adds a feeling of mass and weight to his horses.

The problems of painting the horse in perspective when the artist is a less competent performer than Uccello have resulted in some odd-looking pictures right down to our own day. Horses with long noses, wide-set eyes, narrow-set eyes, no necks, heads disconnected from bodies, enormous hind quarters, etc., frequently appear on the canvases of painters who are highly accomplished at figure painting and landscape. To take a single example, Aelbert Cuyp (1620–91) is a superb painter whose landscapes are illuminated with a wonderfully warm, serene light. He is a skilful draughtsman and his sense of colour is inspired. Yet the horses which frequently appear in his paintings are ungainly. The fact is that many artists can only have regarded horses as part of the 'staffage' in their paintings, whereas to paint them accurately requires special study.

The portrayal of the leaping horse did not present the problem on canvas that was associated with it in sculpture, where the front legs of the horse needed to rest on an object or a crouching figure. Leonardo, who had worked out every conceivable position of man and horse, arrived at a very satisfying composition of a rearing horse whose rider was swinging round in the saddle to deal with a foot soldier beneath him. This posture became a favourite among artists depicting cavalry engagements.

Formal portraiture, however, appeared to require less flamboyant attitudes, and in the portraits of *The Emperor Charles V* by Titian (1488/90–1576) and of *Prince Baltasar Carlos* by Velasquez (1599–1660), both in the Prado, Madrid, the sitters appear slightly as if they were seated on rocking horses (p. 77). Raphael's *St George* in the National Gallery of Art in Washington shares this feeling (p. 72). The attitude of rearing to spring forward may have been based on the experience of the tournament. Despite its slightly archaic composition, Titian's portrait of *The Emperor Charles V* is one of the great painted equestrian portraits. Charles had defeated the Protestants at the battle of Mühlberg in 1547, and the following year he commissioned Titian to paint him leading his army out to battle. The stallion is prancing rather than rearing (a subtle variation), and the Emperor carries a lance and wears magnificent armour. The rich colours of the lowering sky and the intent gaze of the feverish rider bring to the portrait a formidable psychological force comparable with Dürer's *The Knight, Death and the Devil*. The horse in the Titian portrait definitely plays a secondary role and his dark coat is largely covered by a rich tasselled cloth. In the later Velasquez portrait of *Prince Baltasar Carlos*, however, the artist has evidently taken as much pleasure in painting the lively fat little pony as in painting its owner. This remarkable artist has perfectly understood the delineation and foreshortening of the pony as it leaps forward, with its fashionably

flowing mane and tail, across the hills of the Pardo. The young sitter, with a look of inexpressible melancholy and wearing a softly coloured pink sash and green velvet breeches, is seated in a Spanish saddle of the period, a pattern which was exported to the New World and formed a prototype of the Western stock saddle.

With works like the Donatello and Verrocchio sculptures and the Titian painting, equestrian portraiture had reached its zenith, and despite such fine examples as François Clouet's (*c.* 1510–72) painting of *Francis I* and Anthony van Dyck's (1599–1641) of *Charles I* (p. 77), the earlier works were never really surpassed. The genre effectively had nothing more to offer. Formal equestrian portraiture continued, relatively unchanged, through some five centuries, revealing more of changes of fashion in costume and accoutrements than anything else. François Girardon (1628–1715) and Etienne-Maurice Falconet (1716–91) produced masterly bronze statues of Louis XIV and Peter the Great in the Baroque style, and the compositional theme reappears in David's painting of *Bonaparte crossing the Alps* (p. 37). Then the nineteenth century saw a spate of equestrian monuments – mostly of rather mundane quality.

Much greater opportunities were offered to the artist in painting battle scenes in which large numbers of horses and men were caught in violent movement. The imagination of the Renaissance masters was fired by late-Roman scenes like those depicted on Trajan's Column and the Arch of Constantine. The composition for the central theme of Leonardo's lost *Battle of Anghiari* survives in a grisaille copy in the Louvre (p. 79). In it we see all the features which formulated this interpretation of violent action contained within a framework – horses rearing and biting and trampling fallen men, soldiers wielding sabres and fending off blows. Giulio Romano (*c.* 1499–1546) pursued the theme in his *Battle of Constantine* fresco in the Vatican, and the genre perhaps found its most exuberant exponent in Peter Paul Rubens (1577–1640). The movement and surge had a natural appeal to Baroque painters, and in the *Battle of the Amazons* at Munich, Rubens displays a complete mastery of the subject. The seventeenth century witnessed a fashion for small battle scenes and the demand was satisfied by painters such as Jacques Courtois (Il Borgognone, 1621–76), Philips Wouwermans (1619–68) and Jan Wyck (1640–1702). The horses in their compositions were normally too small to require any detailed attention, and their riders, wearing broad-brimmed hats and brandishing muskets and pistolets, were not unlike the riders in Frederic Remington's paintings of the late nineteenth century. These 'furnishing' pictures did not relate to any particular engagement.

The sixteenth century saw a revival in the art of equitation based on scientific principles. Many books appeared up-dating the advice given by Xenophon (431–c. 350 BC) in the first complete treatise *On Horsemanship*, but the method was rationalized and set down by Federico Grisone in his *Gli Ordini de Cavalcare* (The Rules of Horsemanship) in 1561. It was further elaborated by Antoine de Pluvinel and by William Cavendish, Duke of Newcastle (1592–1676) whose *Méthode et Invention Nouvelle de dresser les Chevaux* (*A General System of Horsemanship*) was published in Antwerp in 1657 during the Duke's exile following the Civil War. The book was illustrated by prints after Abraham van Diepenbeck and contains many portraits of the Duke training horses in his riding school, and performing equestrian feats in front of his houses at Welbeck and Bolsover. In two of the plates the Duke finds himself the centre of attraction in a circle of adoring and reverential horses. Before Newcastle felt obliged to leave England after the disastrous Battle of Marston Moor, he had maintained magnificent stables at Welbeck, where no expense was spared to provide every imaginable facility. When one considers that he was estimated to have lost nearly one million pounds as a result of the war, it is possible to imagine the size of this establishment. The Duke built a racecourse near Welbeck after his return to England with Charles II at the Restoration. He subsequently published a second book on horsemanship, *A New Method and Extraordinary Invention to Dress Horses*, in 1667. Apart from the Van Diepenbeck illustrations, the other fine sets of plates depicting dressage include the *Neue Reit-Kunst* by

Johann Elias Ridinger (1698–1767). Individual paintings and engravings illustrating the movements of the *Haute École* were made in the seventeenth and eighteenth centuries. A particularly charming set, to be found at Wilton House, was painted for the tenth Earl of Pembroke by Baron Reis d'Eisenberg, the classical riding master to the court of the Hapsburgs and a talented amateur painter.

The Duke of Newcastle propounded the theory which had already been put forward at the beginning of the seventeenth century by Gervase Markham (1568?–1637): namely, that if you wished to breed racehorses, you should send your English mares to be covered by Barb or Arab stallions. Many Arabian, Turk and Barb horses had been imported into England in the seventeenth and early eighteenth centuries by wealthy men for their studs. The first of the three great Arab stallions, which had been acquired by a Turkish officer, and which was captured at the Siege of Buda in 1688, was brought to England by Captain Byerly. This horse was known as the Byerly Turk. The second, the Darley Arabian, was purchased by Thomas Darley in Aleppo in 1704, and sent to Yorkshire, and the third, the Godolphin Barb, was born in the Yemen and, after passing through the hands of the Bey of Tunis, King Louis XV of France and Edward Coke of Derbyshire, was bought by the second Earl of Godolphin. All Thoroughbred racehorses throughout the world trace their origins, through the General Stud Book, back to these three stallions.

Horse races had been recorded in England since the Middle Ages, but they really became established during the seventeenth century, first during the reign of James I when the Markham Arabian was imported, then more seriously after the Restoration. Charles II's enthusiasm for Newmarket is well known; it was his favourite resort and it was at this period that the character of the sport was established. Spring and autumn meetings were instituted and races were run by professional and amateur jockeys for Royal Plates. The eighteenth century saw even more activity in breeding and racing. The Jockey Club first met in 1752, then in the second part of the century the first classic races were established: the St Leger, the Oaks and the Derby.

Although stag hunting had been prevalent in England for many centuries, the seventeenth century saw fox hunting developing as a major sport. The Quorn Hunt was established in 1698, to be followed in the eighteenth century by the Belvoir and Pytchley, the Beaufort also switching from stag to fox hunting. A major development was the breeding of the modern foxhound. A hound may cover up to eighty miles in one day, and the earlier heavier breeds did not have the stamina for a long run after finding. Greyhounds were often unleashed for this purpose, as witnessed in the Rosebery Gainsborough.

Concurrently with these developments in racing and hunting a new school of painting was emerging in England. Such Church patronage of art as there was ceased to be a factor after the Reformation and Henry VIII's break with Rome. British artists had to seek commissions painting portraits of the royal family and the aristocracy, or painting their possessions: their houses, their horses and sometimes their family pets. Topographical views were occasionally required and even murals, although these latter commissions usually went to foreign artists. There was then no Royal Academy and painters were thought of for the most part as journeymen. It was in this environment that the native English School of animal and sporting painting emerged in the seventeenth and early eighteenth centuries. John Wootton (1683?–1764) was painting landscapes of an Italianate flavour, vaguely in the style of Gaspard Dughet, and he, together with Pieter Tillemans (1684–1734) and Jan Wyck, produced generalized hunting scenes, echoes of Jan Fyt and Frans Snyders and the landscapes of Siberechts. Now, the two sports of racing and hunting created a demand for horse portraits and racing and hunting scenes; a demand which unhappily was not equalled by a tradition of artists trained in these *métiers*. But then the patrons were not looking for works of art. What they demanded was an accurate portrayal and, particularly in horse portraiture, a picture showing the animal's points. Wootton fulfilled this function, as did the talented amateur James Seymour (1702–52) who, perhaps through his independent financial means, escaped the worst aspects of the straitjacket in which his contemporaries found themselves.

The artist who represents the greatest accomplishment of horse painting in eighteenth-century England, but who in fact stands outside the mainstream of its development, is George Stubbs (1724–1806). Lacking any formal training as a painter, Stubbs based his abilities as an artist on a thorough knowledge of anatomy. He must have been a very painstaking man for, after working with Dr Burton, the author of *An Essay Towards a Complete New System of Midwifery*, at York, in his single-mindedness to gain an understanding of the anatomy of the horse he laboriously dissected and made drawings of stinking carcases slung from iron hooks on the ceiling of a deserted farmhouse at Horkstow in Lincolnshire. Up to this time the only authoritative work on the anatomy of the horse was *Dell'Anatomia et dell'Infirmità del Cavallo* (Concerning the Anatomy and the Sickness of the Horse), a sort of equine Vesalius, published in 1598 by Carlo Ruini, a Bolognese amateur anatomist. The appearance of Stubbs's *The Anatomy of the Horse* in 1766, with its twenty-four engraved plates, represented the fruit of over eight years' study and labour. Stubbs's anatomical studies helped him to become one of the greatest masters of form in the eighteenth century. His genius had much in common with that of Leonardo, in that they shared brilliant enquiring minds which embraced both art and science in the mainstream of their thinking. Circumstances, as well as a great intellect, had helped Leonardo to achieve the status of '*Uomo Universale*', and it was ever a source of regret to Stubbs that his abilities inclined his patrons to think of him in connection with horse painting alone. It is difficult today to appreciate the stigma that attached to artists whose subject-matter was not considered elevated. Because horses were regarded as humble objects, Stubbs was placed in the patronising category of 'animal painter'. It is not therefore altogether surprising that his talents were not fully recognized among the artistic fraternity – Füseli called him a 'facsimilist' – and that his genius was more readily appreciated by his scientist friends, the brothers John and William Hunter, and by Joseph Banks, the botanist and President of the Royal Society.

From the sixties Stubbs's horse-painting practice flourished, and it would have been reasonable to expect it to continue to do so for the four

remaining decades of his career. That it didn't may be partly on account of the above-mentioned factor; but also by virtue of his enquiring and experimental approach he turned away partly from horse portraiture and commenced his association with Josiah Wedgwood, and the work on enamel plaques. The scientist and artist in him were seeking new outlets, but oval enamels and a more diversified subject-matter did not prove so acceptable, and his practice declined towards the end of his life.

Some of his finest horse subjects were painted in the sixties and seventies, including *Whistlejacket* and *Gimcrack* (p. 95), when Stubbs had come to number many of the great names of the aristocracy among his patrons, including Rockingham, Grosvenor, Grafton, Bolingbroke, Portland, Torrington and Melbourne. His fertile imagination produced variety in his compositions and, like all great artists, he was capable of painting on a large scale.

Stubbs was too profound and too idiosyncratic an artist to have formed a school. Artists like George Garrard (1760–1826), John Boultbee (*c.* 1745–*c.* 1812) and Abraham Cooper (1787–1868) sometimes painted in his manner, but did not match his genius. One who in some ways does bear comparison, even if of lesser stature, is the Swiss-born Jacques-Laurent Agasse (1767–1849). Agasse studied in Paris under David, arriving in England in 1800. In his work for Lord Rivers, he shows a very real understanding of form in horses. His paintings have an indefinable charm, perhaps attributable to his continental origin.

Two painters with distinct artistic personalities are Ben Marshall (1767–1835) and James Ward (1769–1859). Like Ward, Marshall's style is somewhat mannered, but he was essentially a sporting artist, working for the latter part of his life at Newmarket painting hunting as well as racing subjects. He possessed the ability to describe the muscle and bone structure of horses within the context of a proper understanding of their mass and volume. James Ward was not a sporting artist in the same sense. His painting of *John Levett hunting in the Park at Wychnor* (p. 127) shows that he is quite at home in this genre, but his activities ranged from painting farm animals for the Royal Agricultural Society and landscapes, sometimes in the manner of Rubens, to making

George Stubbs, ARA (1724–1806): *Whistlejacket*, 1761–2

drawings and prints. His long and troubled career continued well into the Victorian era. The romantic side of his many-faceted creativity appealed to Géricault on his visit to London in 1820, and in paintings like his portrait of the racehorse Eagle (p. 126), we can sense the tension and vibrancy which must have impressed the young French artist.

George Morland (1763–1804) clearly, too, had a warm love for horses. The copious output of his short life often featured sympathetically painted tired old greys. The sentimentality which had started to creep in at this stage flowered in the nineteenth century in the work of artists like J. F. Herring (1795–1865) and Edwin Landseer (1802–73). Landseer was a superb draughtsman, but he was also a man of his time. Fortunately, horses do not lend themselves easily to the treatment which dogs received at the hands of a number of Victorian artists, and so we have been spared an equine equivalent of *Dignity and Impudence*.

The boredom of country life in the winter was relieved by hunting. This in turn produced a demand for hunting scenes to decorate the sportsman's parlour. The demand was met by competent if limited painters whose series of *The Meet*, *Going to Covert*, *Full Cry* and *The Death* included an iconographical paraphernalia almost as rigid as that found in medieval illustrations to the New Testament. A literature of hunting sprang up: books as diverse as a serious treatise by Peter Beckford and the lively novels of Robert Surtees with their spirited illustrations by Hablot Browne and John Leech. The characters described were no larger than life, for the period threw up many sporting eccentrics: men like Thomas Worsley who designed his own house as a riding school with accommodation attached, and John Mytton who set fire to his nightshirt to cure himself from an attack of the hiccups. France, too, knew similar devotees; men like the Duc de Condé who wished to be reincarnated as a horse. The Frenchmen Constantin Guys (1802–92) and Jean-Louis Forain (1852–1931) worked in France and England as horse draughtsmen and illustrators to supply a steady if ill-remunerated demand.

Carriages featured on the roads of Europe from an early date. Unsprung wagons pulled by oxen or heavy horses over rough unmade roads were

Jacques-Louis David (1748–1825): *Bonaparte crossing the Alps*, 1800

one of the discomforts to be endured by travellers. Thomas Rowlandson (1756–1827) had a penchant for drawing horse-drawn carriages, and his work reveals the extraordinary variety of vehicles on the road by Regency times. Springs had by then appeared on the lighter forms of transportation, but the best hope of comfort was to travel in the back of a wool carrier's cart. The rapid improvements to carriages in the nineteenth century brought about by specialist coach builders, together with better road surfaces, promoted an interest in driving, and gentlemen kept horses, usually Cleveland Bays, expressly for this purpose. A characteristic picture of this type of equipage is John Ferneley's (1781–1860) *William Massey-Stanley driving his Cabriolet in Hyde Park* (p. 128) painted in 1833.

A short-lived but picturesque development in long-distance transportation was the stage coach. Post horses had long been in existence, but the concept of passenger-carrying vehicles bearing the Royal Mail and cantering past an inn as the coach horn sounded, or one broken down in the snow with a wheel separated from its axle, appealed as readily to the patrons of artists like James Pollard (1797–1859) and Charles Cooper Henderson (1803–77) as they appeal to the purchasers of Christmas cards today. Managing a team of four horses over long distances must have required considerable skill, and the incidents of lost shoes and mechanical breakdown shown in the paintings were all too common, but between 1754 and 1825 the journey time from Manchester to London was reduced from four and a half days to eighteen hours, and this on roads plagued by highwaymen.

For unknown reasons, the horse population had virtually ceased to exist on the American continent when Christopher Columbus landed in Hispaniola (now the Dominican Republic and Haiti). He and subsequent explorers and settlers – Spanish, French, English, Irish, Dutch and German – brought horses with them. A few were left at an early period west of the Mississippi and supposedly started the herds of prairie Mustangs. The Indians, some of whose tribes became highly proficient if somewhat daredevil and cruel horsemen, got their mounts by capturing Mustangs or stealing the white man's. George Catlin (1794–1872), in his naïve paintings of the 1840s, provides a charming and humorous picture of the Indians' relationship with their horses. Some forty years later Frederic Remington (1861–1909) was painting a rather more Hollywood-like scenario.

Racing had been carried on in the American Colonies from before the War of Independence, mostly from imported British bloodstock. English Thoroughbreds were introduced in the early eighteenth century, but the colonists' needs were mainly for hardy, sure-footed animals. Native horses such as the American Quarter Horse, the Standardbred (trotting horse) and Morgan were subsequently bred in the southern states, especially Virginia, Kentucky and Tennessee. The Morgan horse, descended from a bay stallion belonging to a Vermont farmer of that name, is a high-headed cob-like breed which was much favoured by the U.S. Cavalry. The outstanding painter to record American Thoroughbreds was Swiss-born Edward Troye (1808–74), who studied in England for six years before he emigrated to the United States and created paintings in the English idiom for his Kentucky patrons. Puritanism had acted as a brake on Thoroughbred racing, particularly in the north, and this encouraged harness racing, a sport which had developed naturally in the streets. In their quaint fashion, the lithographs of Nathaniel Currier and James Ives, whose partnership flourished from the 1850s, well portray the action of the American trotting horse.

The Napoleonic Wars did not in the final analysis do much to change the map of Europe and the technology of warfare had to await the American Civil War to experience developments wrought by the Industrial Revolution, but the Napoleonic campaigns saw an extended period of movement in Europe. Large armies, foot soldiers and cavalry, swept over Germany, Italy, Poland and Russia, and horses played a major part both in the fighting units and in the baggage and supply trains.

In the field of painting, David's *Bonaparte crossing the Alps* offers nothing new in equestrian portraiture, except perhaps the doubtful quality of melodrama: a scene in which Napoleon is portrayed as the natural successor to Darius, Alexander and Hannibal. Horses featured too in David's classical subjects as incidental to scenes from Roman history in which heroic deeds were designed to inspire the revolutionary. David's pupil, Baron Antoine-Jean Gros (1771–1835), and later Jean-Louis-Ernest Meissonier (1815–91) skilfully employed horses in their military compositions which are, despite the mitigation of the horrors of war, pervaded with a sombre dignity.

The nature of the high-mettled horse rendered it the consummate subject for Romantic painting. The next few decades were to see Eugène Delacroix (1798–1863) and Théodore Géricault (1791–1824), the leading forces in the French Romantic movement, painting horses with such proficiency that they lent an extraordinary dynamic quality to the painters' compositions. Delacroix's visit to Algiers and Morocco in 1832 profoundly impressed him with the colour and exoticism of Islamic Africa. The fruit of this experience is to be seen in such pictures as *The Entry of the Crusaders into Jerusalem* of 1840 in which the fiery Eastern horses form the centrepiece of the composition.

Delacroix's fellow pupil, Géricault, related his short artistic career more directly towards horse painting. His early military pictures, like the *Wounded Cuirassier* of 1814, owe a good deal to Baron Gros, but after the battle of Waterloo he went on an extended visit to Italy. When in Rome during carnival time, he witnessed the riderless horse race, and made a number of paintings of the subject. These scenes, with their counterbalancing forces, supported by skilled lighting effects, possess a potent energy not seen, except perhaps in Goya's *The Second of May, 1808*, since Rubens.

In 1820, Géricault came to England with his painting *The Raft of the Medusa*. With freedom to travel following the Napoleonic Wars, everything English became the rage in France, even more so than in the immediately pre-revolutionary period. Horse racing and its concomitant breeding interests had not taken root as firmly in France as they had done in England. Now Géricault was able to study the work of James Ward and his contemporaries and to paint *The Derby at Epsom* (p. 117).

French racing developed rapidly during the nineteenth century. The Duc d'Orléans built the stables at Chantilly in the thirties and, just after mid-century, the racecourse at Longchamp was added to that at Versailles and augmented with one at Deauville. The demand for horse subjects was met by talented painters like Alfred de Dreux (1810–60) and René Princeteau (1844–1914), but the artist's name inseparable from the French racecourse at this period is that of Edgar Degas (1834–1917).

Degas started painting racing subjects during a stay with friends in Normandy at the age of twenty-seven. Classicism, never far from the surface in French art, reveals itself in his Ingres-like line. He was interested in movement, and ballet dancers and horses provided him with ideal subjects. His work on horses in sculpture, drawing, pastel and painting is always primarily directed towards action and gesture. Eadweard Muybridge's photographic trip-wire experiments had revealed the true movement of the horse at the canter and the gallop, which astonishingly no one had realized before from observation, and Degas was able to investigate in his work the innumerable positions of the horse. Adding to this his absolute grasp of draughtsmanship, his work displays a masterly integrity.

The advent of the railways put paid to the short rule of the stage coach, but more and more horses were required for transportation in cities whose populations swelled relentlessly in the wake of the Industrial Revolution. By 1890 ten thousand horses were needed to draw London's omnibuses and another fifteen thousand for its cabs, quite apart from brewers' dray horses, general carriers, post-office horses, and railway-freight delivery horses. The stabling and foraging requirements were formidable; the removal of manure daunting and unprofitable, once the market gardens surrounding the capital had been surfeited. It was presumably the same in every big city, yet few cared to paint these animals as would almost certainly have been the case a hundred years earlier. Perhaps late-nineteenth-century sentiment, with its requirement for ennobling moral subjects was not in tune, and perhaps the invention of photography had pre-empted the artist's subjects. The

arrival of the internal combustion engine killed off the short-haul horse-drawn vehicle as surely and swiftly as the railway trains had finished the inter-city stage coach. Mechanized agricultural machinery made horses redundant on the farm, and horse power came to have quite another meaning.

After the signing of the Armistice at the conclusion of the First World War, the hundreds of thousands of horses from the field artillery wagon lines were demobilized, together with their brethren at home on the farms and in the cities. The coal which had fuelled industry and the railways was now supplemented by oil for motive power. After some three thousand years the horse was no longer needed, and the utilitarian horse population fell away almost overnight. Where there had been millions there were thousands. Was man's long and intimate relationship with the animal at an end? Fortunately, no. Since the Second World War riding as a recreation has steadily increased in popularity, despite the expense involved. Hunting, pony clubs, horse trials, show jumping and trail riding find an ever-increasing following. In the age of the common man these events are frequently recorded by photography or television – that instant but transient art form.

The relatively sudden change in the 'horse economy' was accompanied by revolutionary changes in the field of art. By many, representational art was considered to have run its course, and a number of movements, all in some degree abstracted from realist painting, have resulted. In this context, Picasso (1881–1973) was inspired to paint a horse as an abstract linear concept in *Guernica*, to the sore distress of Sir Alfred Munnings (1878–1959) whose work is an updated version of the nineteenth-century idiom. Patronage too has changed, with the arrival of official committees who are perhaps inclined to be more 'adventurous' in spending the money placed under their control than are private individuals who are paying out of their own pockets. We are now in the curious situation of seeing modern artists with established reputations like Marino Marini (b. 1901), who has a predilection for representing horses albeit in somewhat abstracted form, working concurrently with contemporary artists like John Skeaping (b. 1901),

LEFT Edgar Degas (1834–1917):
Steeplechase . . . The Fallen Jockey, 1866

RIGHT Marino Marini
(b. 1901): *Horse*

whose equestrian bronze sculpture is, for want of a better word, classical. Both are making a valid artistic statement.

What of the future? Our natural resources under the soil are fast running out and our technology has not yet begun to provide a viable alternative. Simple-minded romantics will doubtless be envisaging a return to the past, yet who would want to see horses bred to lead the squalid existence they had to suffer in urban areas in the latter half of the nineteenth century?

The artistic movements, which have proliferated in more recent years, following the departure from traditional styles of painting established at the time of the Renaissance, have for the most part been movements of ideas. Horse painting does not lend itself to this sort of interpretation, but depends absolutely on the artist having a proper understanding of the animal's form and structure. The horse is in itself a work of art and any attempt to sublimate it must be based on knowledge; a case of 'truth is beauty'.

The second factor accounting for today's uncertainty is loss of religious confidence in the face of technology, Horses once held a slightly mystical connotation for man. Physically, with their perfect movement, they seemed to contain an element of divinity. Seated astride them one could move at great speed – almost fly. What does that mean now to the motorway driver. Yet there *is* a difference, and perhaps when we have come to terms with scientific advancement we shall gain a better sense of values. Hopefully, this might bring a new confidence – another re-birth bringing with it new creative artistic activity. As it is, we have to look back to the past to find the best interpretations of horses in art, and we are most fortunate in still having a wonderful inheritance, including such masterpieces as the T'ang burial horses, the bronze horses from St Mark's, Leonardo's horse studies, and the great canvases of George Stubbs.

One thing is certain: there will always be men and women, some with an artist's eye, who keep horses close to their hearts, and who identify in the animal's make-up a sense of freedom, strength and nobility.

ABOVE *Pharoah Seti I* (*c.* 1305–1290 BC)
in a war Chariot; detail of a stone carving from
the temple of Amun at Karnak, Egyptian,
1st millennium BC
RIGHT *Archer and Charioteer*; bas-relief
from Carchemish in Northern Syria,
Neo-Hittite, 9th century BC
OPPOSITE *King Tiglath-pileser III*
(745–727 BC) *standing in his Chariot under
a Parasol*; bas-relief from the palace of
Nimrud, Assyrian, 8th century BC

In the ancient world the Near and Middle
East were involved in a continuous power
struggle, with successive rulers establishing
empires of more or less hegemony, supported
by armies and maintained by tribute exacted
through terror. Horse-drawn chariots,
providing speed and manoeuvrability,
played a significant role in their wars.

THE HORSE IN ANCIENT CIVILIZATIONS

LEFT ABOVE *Horse on a Stand*, Greek, 750–700 BC
LEFT BELOW *Horse and Rider*, Greek, *c*. 500 BC
ABOVE *Mounted Cavalryman*, Greek, *c*. 550 BC

The two unsophisticated statuettes on the left both betray a complete absence of anatomical understanding. The bronze *Horse on a Stand* dates from the 'geometric' period of Greek art and is said to have come from Olympia. By this time the Mycenean civilization had vanished, yet artistic activity shone through the dark period that followed. The *Horse and Rider* was probably made as a child's toy and would have been hand painted; it was found at Tanagra, near Thebes.

The quality of the beautiful little bronze cavalryman and horse indicates a marked development in horse sculpture achieved in a relatively short period. The general conformation and proportions of the animal are well described. It was found at Grumentum in southern Italy and was probably made by a member of the Greek colony established there.

Bronze helmet, Greek, *c.* 600 BC

Horses have always lent status to their owners, although the rocky, dry nature of the Greek countryside has never been sympathetic to riding or grazing them. The importance of cavalry was demonstrated at the battle of Marathon in 490 BC but in the seventh and sixth centuries BC the Greek City States had to rely mainly on their heavily armed hoplites, or foot soldiers.
The helmet, found at Arkanes in Crete, would have belonged to a wealthy horse-owning hoplite.

45

LEFT Head of a horse from the chariot of Selene, goddess of the moon, from the east pediment of the Parthenon, Greek, 5th century BC
ABOVE Detail of a battle scene from the *Alexander Sarcophagus*, Greek, 4th century BC
ABOVE RIGHT *A Rearing Horse*, South Italy, *c*. AD 50

The sculpture from the Parthenon portrays the moon goddess's exhausted horse at the close of night. Originally it formed a moving contrast with the freshness of the sun god's team placed opposite.

The carvings from the *Alexander Sarcophagus*, while not displaying the superb quality of the marbles from the Parthenon, are nevertheless a tribute to the level of artistic accomplishment achieved in provincial centres by the fourth century BC. The connection of the sarcophagus with Alexander is quite apocryphal. It was probably commissioned by a family of Persian noblemen and made in one of the Greek islands. It was found at Sidon, north of Tyre, on the eastern seaboard of the Mediterranean.

The small bronze statue of a rearing horse, with its unusual bridle, was found in the ancient city of Herculaneum during the excavations in the eighteenth century. Herculaneum had disappeared in AD 79 under a torrent of volcanic mud accompanying the disastrous eruption of Vesuvius.

FAR LEFT Detail of a bronze horse from St Mark's Cathedral, Venice, Roman, *c.* 400–200 BC
LEFT *Amazons on Horseback*, Etruscan, late 6th century BC
BELOW *A Vandal Landowner*, North Africa, *c.* AD 500
BELOW RIGHT *A four-horse Chariot* (Quadriga) *approaching the Goals*, Roman, 1st century AD
RIGHT *A two-horse Chariot* (Biga), Roman, 1st–2nd century AD

The four famous bronze horses, prominently located above the entrance to St Mark's Cathedral, exercised a profound influence, together with the statue of Marcus Aurelius (p. 29), on Renaissance equestrian sculpture. The horses were transported from Constantinople in 1204, following the city's defeat at the hands of the Crusaders supported by the Doge Enrico Dandolo, and were taken to Venice.

The Amazon riders portrayed on the silver panel with gold sections were known to ancient civilizations as a tribe of female warriors from the Black Sea district – a concept that caught the imagination of successive generations of artists.

North Africa and Andalusia had native horse populations from early times whose origins were lost in obscurity and the horse illustrated in the mosaic was probably a local one.

The two models of Roman chariots bear witness to the popularity of chariot racing which reached its peak in the later days of the Roman Empire.

THE EARLY ORIENTAL HORSE

Head of a Horse, Chinese, 6 Dynasties (AD 222–589)

The Ancient East's geographical and cultural isolation led to
a separate artistic development from that of the West.
Most of the early figures of horses that have been found
in the East were made to be buried in the tombs of the dead.

RIGHT ABOVE *Horse*, Chinese, 6 Dynasties (AD 22?–589)
RIGHT BELOW *Horse*, Chinese, late 6th–early 8th century AD
FAR RIGHT *Equestrian Figure*, Chinese, T'ang Dynasty (AD 618–906)

The squat terracotta horse, with a high-backed saddle, is typical of the Mongolian ponies prevalent in China prior to the introduction of Western blood during the Han Dynasty. Stirrups were introduced on military horses during the fourth century in both the Eastern and Western worlds.

The high-backed saddle common in early China can again be seen in the provincial rendering of a more Western-style horse from Astana cemetery in north-west China. In an attempt to create a realistic appearance, the horse has been painted with dapples and been given a tuft of forelock.

In the equestrian figure, a burial piece, the artist has achieved a refinement which is quite absent from the other two models. The unglazed terracotta would have been painted.

ABOVE *Horses with Grooms*, Chinese, T'ang Dynasty
(AD 618–906)
OPPOSITE Horse's head in the form of a silver rhyton,
Persian, Sassanian Dynasty (AD 224–642)

Among some early tribes such as the Scythians, when a leader died, his
horses were killed and buried with him. As civilization developed this
extravagant practice was abandoned, and models were made instead to be
interred with the dead. The period of the Han Dynasty (206 BC–AD 222)
in China saw the improvement of such pottery models, but they reached
their most beautiful form in the T'ang Dynasty. These characteristic
glazed figures of horses from the tomb of T'ing hsun are accompanied by
their attendants. The expectation was that they would be re-animated
to serve the dead man in the after-life.

The silver drinking vessel is an epitaph to the skills of the Sassanian
silversmiths. During the Sassanian Dynasty in Persia – where a man's
wealth was reckoned by the number of horsemen he had at his disposal –
there was a further movement away from Hellenistic towards Oriental art
as the influence of Greek craftsmen following the train of Alexandrian
conquest declined.

...URA:AN GLORUM EXER ACITU:

THE MEDIEVAL HORSE AND THE AGE OF CHIVALRY

LEFT Detail of Norman cavalry from *The Bayeux Tapestry*, 11th century
ABOVE Giovanni di Paolo (*c.* 1403–*c.* 1482): *The Triumph of Death*, 1450–60?

In medieval times heavy horses were bred for warfare and jousting, but the dominance of the Church and the preponderance of religious themes discouraged the inclusion of horses in art.

The events of the battle of Hastings, which brought Anglo-Saxon England to a sudden end, are recorded on the famous two-hundred-and-thirty-feet-long embroidery at Bayeux. To some extent the victory of the Normans can be attributed to the fact that their cavalry rode on light unprotected horses giving them great mobility while King Harold's army consisted primarily of foot soldiers wielding the old-fashioned two-handled Viking axes. This was the first time in Western Europe that an invading army had transported its horses across the sea; the Norman knights needed chargers specially bred and trained to carry them.

In the fifteenth-century miniature Death, bearing the appurtenances of Time and the Devil, approaches his victim astride a scrawny-looking jade. Death was never far from men's minds in the Middle Ages and the artist here has been at pains to give the horse an underfed, spectral appearance.

ABOVE The Master of the Housebook (active 1465–1500): *Wild Men Jousting*
LEFT *The Lion and the Horse*; an illustration from Aesop's *Leben und Fabeln*, Augsburg, 1479

In these two illustrations originating from the Rhine region both artists have allowed their imagination free rein. *Aesop's Fables*, which are centred on animals, were enormously popular in the fifteenth century and the last three decades of the century saw the publication of well over a hundred editions.

The Sienese commissioned Simone
Martini's painting in 1328 to
commemorate the victory of the
condottiere Guidoriccio da Fogliano
over Castruccio Castraceni.
The Sienese commander is seen astride
his grey inspecting his defences on the
eve of the battle. Despite the dreamy
quality of the artist's interpretation
of the scene, the elaborately
decorated mantle which envelops the
horse and the matching raiment of
the rider are probably accurate
representations.

   The Italian drawing, separated by
over a hundred and twenty years
from Simone Martini's painting,
shows that the elaborate trappings of
the horses, necessary for their
protection in combat, were still a
prominent feature of courtly life.
By the fifteenth century, jousting
had largely taken the place of
mounted combat between gentlemen. Although lives were spared,
tournaments allowed plenty of scope
for the aggressive spirit. Prizes
included the chance of winning the
admiration of a wealthy heiress, and
penalties the possibility of staking
and losing one's horse and
accoutrements.

FAR LEFT Lucas Cranach the Elder
(1472–1553): *St George on Horseback
with the dead Dragon*, 1507
LEFT Hans Burgkmair (1473–1559):
The Emperor Maximilian I on Horseback, 1508
RIGHT Benozzo Gozzoli (1420–97):
The Journey of the Magi to Bethlehem, 1463

The two woodcuts illustrate the
magnificent armour, more ceremonial
than practical, worn by leading noblemen
of the period and the type of heavy horse,
strong enough to carry it, which they rode.
These rich woodcuts were individually
printed in gold and black with more than
one block on tinted paper, probably for
presentation.

Gozzoli has also mounted his princes on
the romantic white chargers beloved by
artists of the time. He has seized the
opportunity provided by the subject to
paint a cavalcade of distinguished men
and their ladies, among them members of
the Medici family and the Emperor John
Palaeologus, in contemporary dress.

LEFT Antonio Pisanello (1395–1455): *The Vision of St Eustace*, 1436–8
RIGHT Albrecht Dürer (1471–1528): *The Vision of St Eustace*, *c.* 1501

The subject of these two images – the saint who while hunting in the forest saw a vision of Christ appear between a deer's antlers – provided ideal material for the artist who needed an excuse for painting horses. Pisanello's painting was attributed to Dürer until the end of the nineteenth century, but in fact Dürer based his engraving on the Pisanello composition. Pisanello's portrayal of a heavy horse in a dark medieval forest is similar in mood to Uccello's *The Hunt* (p. 31).

Dürer's print, although superficially very similar to Pisanello's painting, is quite different. A subtle composition of arches and curves winds upwards into a little medieval hill town. The saint has dismounted and the hounds are disposed in such a way as to effect maximum realism. The horse is of a lighter breed than Pisanello's and could be the same model as that used by Dürer in his *Soldier on Horseback* (p. 69).

LEFT René d'Anjou (1409–80):
Tournament Ceremonial from *Traité
de la Forme et Devis d'un Tournois*
RIGHT The Limbourg brothers (active
first half of the 15th century): *August*
from *Les Très Riches Heures du Duc de Berry*
FAR RIGHT *Ploughing Scene*, Flemish, 1416

Three beautiful miniatures which
emphasize the essential role of the horse in
the daily life of both rich and poor in the
Middle Ages. The Duke of Anjou was a
knowledgeable enthusiast of the
tournament as well as being a talented
amateur painter. The Limbourg brothers
have created an air of unreality set in an
arcadian golden age in their miniature
showing an aristocratic party of falconers
returning to their castle.

The activities shown in the ploughing
scene hardly changed until the
agricultural tractor replaced the farm
horse in the present century. The horses
draw a plough in the middle distance
while in the foreground a peasant with
a whip urges on two horses harnessed
to a harrow. The collar and blinkers are
easily recognizable, although the horses, if
in proportion to the driver, are
considerably smaller than nineteenth-
century English Shire horses.

63

LEFT Paolo Uccello (1396/7–1475):
Monument to Sir John Hawkwood, 1425–36
ABOVE Paolo Uccello:
St George and the Dragon, c. 1455
RIGHT Paolo Uccello:
The Battle of San Romano, 1435–50

Uccello loved to include animals in his pictures
and he was one of the earliest Renaissance painters
to concentrate on the horse. He was responsible for

establishing three-dimensional perspective in
painting, often using his monumental-style horses
to demonstrate his theories.

In 1436 the Cathedral authorities in Florence
commissioned him to paint a fresco as a
monument to Sir John Hawkwood, the great
condottiere, who had died in 1394. The battle of
San Romano was a minor engagement fought
on 1 July 1432 between the Florentines
and the Sienese.

FAR LEFT Donatello (c. 1386–1466): *The Gattamelata Monument*, 1443–53
LEFT Antonio Pollaiuolo (1433–98): *Study for an Equestrian Monument to Francesco Sforza, c.* 1490
RIGHT Leonardo da Vinci (1452–1519): *Studies for the Trivulzio Monument*, 1508–11

Donatello was commissioned, probably by the Venetian Senate, to design a monument to the military commander Erasmo da Narni, known as Gattamelata (The Tiger Cat). The latter's death in 1443 was seized on as an opportunity to create an equestrian statue to compare with the monuments of antiquity. The statue of Marcus Aurelius (p. 29) and the bronze horses of St Mark's (p. 48) are the obvious prototypes.

Pollaiuolo and Leonardo were less successful with designs for a projected statue to Francesco Sforza, Duke of Milan from 1450 to 1497. Their inspiration derived from the free movement they had observed in the battle scenes carved in relief on classical sarcophagi, and the commission went to Leonardo. Leonardo made a number of preliminary drawings but the statue was never executed.

Leonardo's sketch on the right shows three variants for another abortive scheme, on this occasion to build a sepulchral monument incorporating an equestrian figure for the Milanese commander Trivulzio.

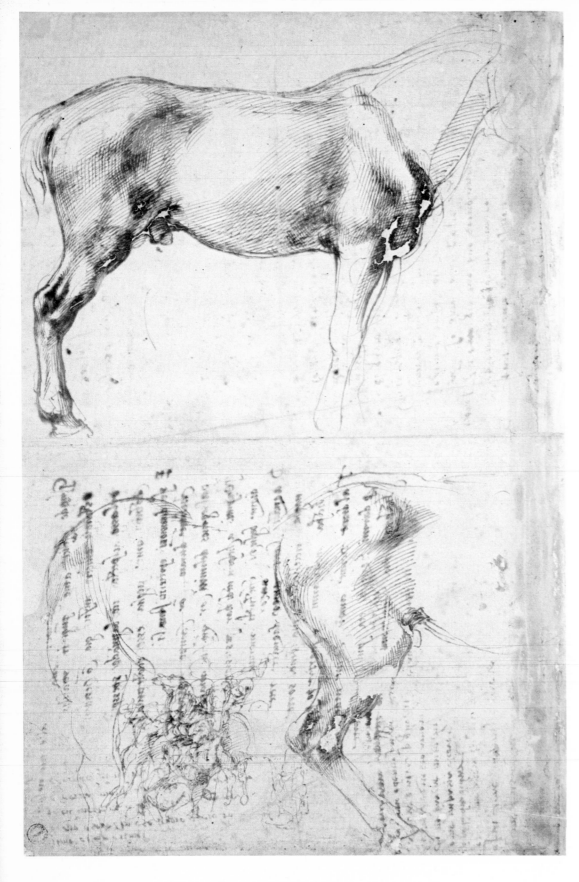

FAR LEFT Michelangelo (1475–1564): *Studies of a Horse, and a Horseman attacking Foot Soldiers, c.* 1505
LEFT Antonio Pisanello (1395–1455): *Two Horses, c.* 1436–8
RIGHT Albrecht Dürer (1471–1528): *St George,* 1508
FAR RIGHT Albrecht Dürer: *Soldier on Horseback with a Lance,* 1498

Renaissance artists were partially liberated from the stricter confines of religious painting; they turned to pure interpretation of form using classical art as their example.

Michelangelo's horse studies are clearly drawn from life. For an artist almost wholly preoccupied with the human figure, he shows a remarkable understanding of the animal's form.

Pisanello's two horses, wearing saddles and bridles characteristic of the period, were probably studies for his fresco of *St George and the Dragon* in Sant'Anastasia, Verona.

Dürer's engraving of a mounted saint presents the medieval ideal of chivalry, while his watercolour, almost certainly taken from life, portrays a much more truthful version of the reality of a soldier's life. Dürer used the drawing fifteen years later as a model for the horse in his engraving *The Knight, Death and the Devil* (p. 27).

Dz ist die rüstung zw der zeit
mi tewtzschlant gewest

1498

ABOVE Lambert Doomer (1623–1700): *Two Farm Horses*
ABOVE RIGHT Attributed to Roelant Savery (1576–1639): *A Two-horse Team*, 1559–63

Both the sympathetic studies of farm horses are clearly drawn from life and are typical of
the growing awareness of the horse as a subject worthy of study in its own right rather than
purely as an adjunct to a more elevated theme.

ABOVE Hans Baldung Grien (1484/5–1545): *A Stallion in a Herd of Wild Horses*, 1534
RIGHT Piero di Cosimo (1462–1521): *Allegory*, c. 1500

Two images where the artists have introduced fantasy rather than realism into
their compositions. Some, however, who have watched horses fighting may not think that
Hans Baldung has exaggerated their behaviour in this close-knit, violent scene.

LEFT Raphael (1483–1520):
St George and the Dragon, 1504–5
ABOVE Raphael: *Head of a Horse, c.* 1511

Raphael's beautiful little panel – an archaically
conceived representation of a prancing white
charger – was painted for the Duke of Guidobaldo
da Montefeltro and was later taken to England and
given to Henry VII. The drawing is a fragment of
the cartoon for the fresco *The Expulsion of Heliodorus*.

ABOVE Rinaldo Montovano and Benedetto Pagni (pupils of Giulio Romano,
c. 1499–1546): detail of fresco decorations in the Sala dei Cavalli at
the Palazzo del Té, Mantua, 1527–8
RIGHT Giovanni Bologna or Giambologna (1529–1608): *Horse Prancing*, 1581

The fresco decorations show six horses in all – three dapple grey, two chestnut
and one dark grey – beneath representations of the Labours of Hercules.
The handsome stallions are portraits of horses from the Gonzaga family's
nearby stables. During the Renaissance the great Italian families developed
their own outstanding breeds – each trying to outdo their rivals by
producing faster and more beautiful animals.

FAR LEFT El Greco
(1540/50–1614): *St Martin and
the Beggar*, 1604–14
LEFT Caravaggio (*c.* 1562–1609):
The Conversion of St Paul, 1600–1
RIGHT Titian (1488/90–1576):
A Horse and Rider falling
FAR RIGHT Lelio Orsi
(1511–87): *A Man holding
a rearing Horse*

The horses are crucial to
the composition of the two
paintings commemorating
celebrated events in Christian
history. El Greco's inexperience
in painting horses is evident in
his late picture: the animal
seems disjointed and a sense of
of volume is not properly
conveyed. Caravaggio's
painting describes the dramatic
moment during St Paul's
journey to Damascus when
'there shined round about him
a light from heaven: and he fell
to the earth'. The contrast
between St Paul's quiet mount,
held by a servant, and the
prostrate rider is emphasized
by brilliant chiaroscuro.
  Titian's drawing was
probably a study for his
painting, *The Battle of Cadore*.
In both drawings the man
appears to be losing control
of his horse; Orsi's design
revolves around the battle of
strength between the two.

75

LEFT Charles le Brun (1619–90):
The Chancellor Siguier, 1660
RIGHT Sir Anthony van Dyck (1599–1641):
Charles I on Horseback, late 1630s
FAR RIGHT Diego Velasquez (1599–1660):
Prince Baltasar Carlos, 1635–6

Le Brun's sympathetic portrait shows his loyal patron Chancellor Siguier astride a fine heavy horse with the long mane and forelock which were so fashionable at the time. Siguier paid for Le Brun to visit Italy where he was favourably received and employed by Cardinal Barberini and Pope Urban VIII. He later returned to France to be immensely successful under the patronage of Louis XIV. Le Brun's slightly florid style, unfashionable in painting today, was perfectly in tune with the period.

In the portrait of Charles I, Van Dyck has chosen a low viewpoint in order to accentuate the size of the rider in relationship to his mount; this was a necessary device as the king was a very small man. Van Dyck adopted the pose of the horse and rider from Titian's *Charles V before the Battle of Mühlberg* (p. 33) but has placed much more importance on the horse in his composition.

Velasquez has created a masterly image of the fresh fat little pony with its sad-faced, short-lived rider. It is all the more remarkable in that he painted the pony after it had died and been stuffed.

FAR LEFT Sir Anthony van Dyck:
*Charles I on Horseback with
M. de St Antoine*, 1633
LEFT Sir Peter Paul Rubens
(1577–1640): *A Knight of
the Golden Fleece, c.* 1610
RIGHT Sir Peter Paul Rubens:
copy after *The Battle of Anghiari,
c.* 1600–8

Pierre Antoine Bourdin, Seigneur de
St Antoine, a master of horsemanship,
had been sent to James I of England by
Henri IV of France with a gift of six horses
and a letter recommending him as *'un
escuier choisy de ma main'* (a horseman chosen
by my own hand). Charles I retained him
and in Van Dyck's painting we see Bourdin,
thirty years later, preceding the king's horse.
   Rubens's paintings provide the
quintessence of the Baroque style; the
flowing manes and tails of his curvaceous
horses bear no relation to reality. His copy
of *The Battle of Anghiari* is one of the
few records we have of Leonardo's
lost fresco, commissioned in 1503,
the subject matter of which centred
on fighting horsemen.

LEFT Stefano della Bella (1610–64):
Stag Hunt
RIGHT John Vanderbank (1696–1739):
A Man on Horseback, 1728
FAR RIGHT Adrien van der Venne
(1589–1662): *A Man on Horseback*, *c.* 1625?

Della Bella was primarily an etcher who
started his career by imitating the work of
Jacques Callot, echoes of whose style were
always present in his work. What really
brings Della Bella his individuality is his
love of animals, particularly horses, and
they appear in large numbers in his prolific
output. His practised hand and flowing line
imply movement and form, as in the
hunting scene where the rider is poised in
the saddle, about to throw his spear.

   Vanderbank was a minor English artist
who frequently introduced horses into his
work; his understanding of the animal
produces an easy balanced poise. He has
adopted the same pose for his drawing of a
horse and rider as that used by Van Dyck in
his portrait of *Charles I on Horseback with
M. de St Antoine* (p. 78). Van der Venne
has produced a naturalistic study of the
same subject, less stylized than the
Vanderbank; it must give a very truthful
impression of a seventeenth-century
Dutchman out riding on his hack.

FAR LEFT Aelbert Cuyp
(1620–91): *Lady and Gentleman
on Horseback, c.* 1660
LEFT Philips Wouwermans
(1619–68): *The Grey*
RIGHT Rembrandt van Rijn
(1606–69): *The Polish Rider,* 1655

The two naturalistic paintings of
horses on the left are characteristic
of the Dutch style of art in the
seventeenth century. The head
and shoulders of the lady's grey
mount in Cuyp's beautiful
painting are very disproportionate
to the body; perhaps the artist was
trying to prevent the horse's head
being more significant than
the sitter's.

   Rembrandt's enigmatic and
rather mysterious subject does
not appear to have any specific
Polish connection, but his dress
may be that of some East
European light cavalry engaged
in the endless struggle against the
infidel. Horses sometimes appear
in Rembrandt's work as occasion
requires, but apart from the
Portrait of an Officer on Horseback in
the National Gallery, London,
this is the nearest we have to
a horse portrait from him.

LEFT Detail of *The Samurai Captain Kumagai Naozane pursuing his Enemy during the Battle of Ichinotani, 1184*, Japanese, 17th century
ABOVE *Mongol mounted Archer*, Chinese, Ming Dynasty (1386–1644)

In later Eastern art miniature painting was much favoured and horses featured in narrative subjects.

The Japanese screen painting illustrates a scene from a famous Samurai legend. The Mongolian pony in the Chinese drawing is typical of the breed that had been prevalent in the East for centuries.

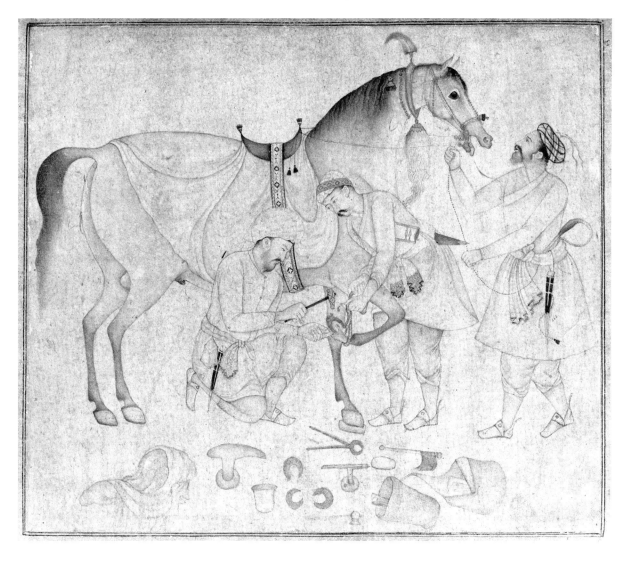

ABOVE *A Stallion being Shod, c.* 1600, India, Mughal School
RIGHT *Hawking, c.* 1725, India, Mughal School

The farrier's tools are displayed in the foreground of the Mughal drawing. The hawking miniature is a late example of the idiom before the Mughal court succumbed to British authority.

جرا ساختی بیده و مکروفریب | شادی چنین هرکه آیبین من | وکه جنک ازین وکابلستان | جایدم از جنک زابلستان | همانا ندیدی تنکی نشیب | جهاندار تاج برتر نهر | کشتن دهم

نزانیت این کار در دین | کزایشان یکی زنده کردن | تا کرزهمی یاد باید بیای | منم بیش زو هرکه جنک آیدم | خودایندجهان تاج برتر نهر

مرا یا زهرکذر تا زبکار | را یا زهرکذر تا نا یدبیای

LEFT *The Combat between Rustam and Isfandiar*, Persian School, 14th century
RIGHT *A Horse rising to its Feet*, Chinese, K'ang-Hsi Dynasty (1662–1722)
FAR RIGHT *A Prince receiving Water at a Well, c.* 1700, India, Mughal School

The Persian miniature is from the *Shāh-Nāmah* (The Book of Kings), a history of the kings of Persia written in the tenth century by Firdausi and

یاد دنجت اکردان بود | شن وکاراز ایتخت خلان بود | توجنت جوی و منم جنک خواه | بکردیم یک بادکنی خواه | به بنیم نا اسب اسفندیار | نوی آخر آیدهمی سوار

کن بان بایم پشت جکوی | ماوان بهدیدی خدا وندوی | نهادندهمان دوجنک که کز | ناشدیان جنک فادزدن | خستنه ، شنه را آمدزد | همی خون شون فرورجخنتد

successively re-written and re-illustrated over the centuries. The edition from which the illustration comes – the *Demotte Shāh-Nāmah* – was painted after the Mongol invasion; the Mongolian-style ponies ridden by the combatants bear witness to the influx of this foreign culture. The Chinese earthenware pony is also of the Mongolian type; it has been over-glazed in a rich yellow enamel.

Although the Mughal Empire traced its origins back to Timur and Genghis Khan, the school of painting only originated, and matured very rapidly, during the reign of Akbar (1542–1605).

The miniature shows a prince, richly dressed, receiving a bowl of water from one of three ladies at a well. In painting the lower part of the horse orange, the artist may be presumed to be shunning reality in favour of exotic fantasy while illustrating a romance.

THE EIGHTEENTH CENTURY

Childers.

LEFT James Seymour (1702–52):
*Flying Childers galloping to the Left,
bridled but not saddled, c.* 1739
RIGHT James Seymour:
Flying Childers with Jockey up, 1740

The eighteenth century was the
classical period of horse portraiture in
England. It also saw the development
and perfection of the Thoroughbred.

Flying, or Devonshire, Childers was
bred by Colonel Leonard Childers and
foaled in 1715. He was out of Betty
Leeds whose dam, Cream Cheeks, was
by the Leeds Arabian, and he himself
was the great-grandsire of Eclipse.
Flying Childers was bought by the
second Duke of Devonshire for whom
he raced with great success.

The drawing is of particular interest
showing as it does Seymour's working
methods. A very prolific horse
draughtsman, Seymour has completed
his working study in every detail except
for such items as the saddle, saddle
cloths and the rider. These were then
added when the painting was executed
later in the studio.

FLYING CHILDERS

LEFT
James Seymour:
*The Kill at
Ashdown Park*, 1743
RIGHT
Pieter Tillemans
(1684–1734):
*View of the Round
Course at Newmarket,
with Racehorses
going to the Start for
the King's Plate,
c.* 1720

Seymour's painting
shows Lord Craven,
accompanied by
huntsmen and
hounds, gathered
round for the Kill
before the gates of
Ashdown Park on
the Berkshire Downs.
In the ambitious
composition we find,
in primitive and
naïve form, echoes of
Uccello's perspective
devices.

In Tillemans's
painting of racing
at Newmarket, the
central figure on the
grey could be George I.

In some ways Seymour's painting of Sir Roger Burgoyne is the epitome of English sporting horse portraiture: the country gentleman is shown with his most prized possessions. The tradition is continued in the nineteenth century in such pictures as H.B. Chalon's *A Groom with a Bay*

Hunter in a Park (p. 121) and in our own century with Sir Alfred Munnings's *My Wife, my Horse and Myself*.

Seymour's charming interior invokes a composition which was much repeated, with variations, until well into the nineteenth century.

Wootton was the first distinguished English sporting painter. His portraits of horses are records of a great age of horse breeding. The large canvas with its scene of violent tension was painted to be hung high up on the wall at Longleat in Wiltshire and must have tested his abilities to the full.

George Stubbs, ARA (1724–1806): *Hambletonian being rubbed down, with a Trainer and a Stable-lad*, 1799

Hambletonian, by King Fergus out of Highflyer, was a descendant of Eclipse. He was foaled in 1792 and won the St Leger in 1795. When an eight-year-old he was raced at the Newmarket Craven meeting as the property of Sir Harry Vane-Tempest against

Mr Joseph Cookson's Diamond for a wager of three thousand guineas. Starting at odds of five to one, Hambletonian just managed to win having been mercilessly whipped to the finish. Vane-Tempest then commissioned Stubbs to paint the horse, which was never run again. The artist was subsequently forced to sue the owner for payment. Stubbs's powers were undiminished at the age of seventy-five when he painted this horse portrait.

George Stubbs: *Gimcrack on Newmarket Heath with
a Trainer, Jockey and Stable-lad*, 1765

Gimcrack, by Cripple out of Blossom, was foaled in 1760 and first raced at Epsom in 1764.
The painting was commissioned from Stubbs in 1765 by Gimcrack's owner, the second Viscount
Bolingbroke. Stubbs shows the horse twice, being rubbed down in the foreground, and winning a race
by several lengths in the distance. Gimcrack won twenty-seven out of his thirty-five starts.

Newmarket, scene of so many horse portraits of the eighteenth century, became
the centre for horse racing during the reign of Charles II, that passionate supporter
of the Turf. Its geographical position, equally accessible both to London and
the breeding grounds of the Midlands, helped to confirm its supremacy. In the
eighteenth century the Jockey Club set up its headquarters there and fashioned
the English Turf institutions which were to provide a model for all other countries
in which horse racing became popular.

LEFT George Stubbs: *Racehorses belonging to the Duke of Richmond exercising at Goodwood*, 1760–1
ABOVE Thomas Sandby, RA (1723–98): *The New North Face of Great Lodge*, c. 1760

Painted for the third Duke of Richmond, Stubbs's picture must have been one of his first commissions after he moved south in about 1759 from Lincolnshire where he had been working on the dissection and drawing of the horse. On the left of the painting, the Duke, his wife Mary and his sister-in-law, Lady Louisa Lennox, can be seen, all mounted.

In the foreground of the painting of the Great Lodge, now Cumberland Lodge, in Windsor Great Park the Stud Groom Barnard Smith is lunging a colt, watched on the right by the Duke of Cumberland and three attendant gentlemen.

LEFT George Stubbs:
Portrait of a Racehorse:
Otho with Jockey up, 1766
RIGHT George Stubbs:
Portrait of a Racehorse:
Turf with Jockey up, c. 1765

The two horse portraits, with
Stubbs's favourite Newmarket
Heath background,
are excellent examples of
the work he was doing in the
later sixties and the seventies
when his sporting
patronage was at its height.

OVERLEAF George Stubbs:
detail of *Mares and Foals
without a Background*, 1762

One of a group of nine extant
paintings where Stubbs has
contrived a balanced frieze-
type composition in which he
is able to place horses in
various postures. The absence
of a background in this version,
painted for the second
Marquis of Rockingham,
focuses attention entirely
on the horses.

ABOVE George Stubbs:
The Prince of Wales's Phaeton, 1793
ABOVE RIGHT George Stubbs:
Soldiers of the 10th Light Dragoons, 1793

Two paintings commissioned by the
Prince of Wales, later George IV.
The painting above shows Thomas, the
royal coachman, holding one of the two
harnessed carriage horses, while a boy
holds the carriage shaft. The Prince's dog

Fino jumps up at the second horse.
The second painting shows two sergeants,
a trumpeter and a private from
the Prince's regiment, the 10th Light
Dragoons. Dragoons were a rather
cumbrous musket-bearing cavalry.

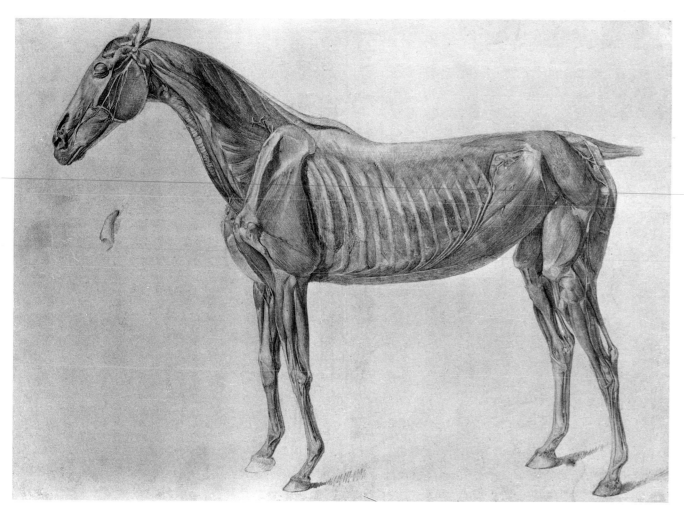

ABOVE George Stubbs:
Flayed Horse, 1758–9
ABOVE RIGHT George Stubbs:
Portrait of the Racehorse Rufus, 1762–7

Stubbs's drawing shows the side view of a flayed horse, the outer layers of the muscles having been removed. It is a study for his engraved work, *The Anatomy of the Horse*, published in 1766, the fruit of the many months he spent in isolation dissecting and drawing horses. The lessons that he had absorbed from his study of the anatomy of the horse are evident in his portrait of the racehorse Rufus.

LEFT George Stubbs: *Horse attacked by a Lion*, 1769
RIGHT George Stubbs: *Horse frightened by a Lion*, 1770

The subjects of the two pictures are known in several
variants and are possibly adapted from the theme of an
antique sculpture which Stubbs saw in the courtyard of
the Palazzo Senatorio in Rome during his visit to the
city in 1754.

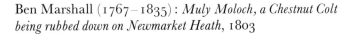

Ben Marshall (1767–1835): *Muly Moloch, a Chestnut Colt being rubbed down on Newmarket Heath*, 1803

By the time the portrait of Muly Moloch was painted, Marshall had established himself as one of the leading sporting artists of the day and had acquired a worthwhile clientèle. He settled in Newmarket for many years in order to be better able to study and paint the horse. The stable-lad who is holding Muly Moloch beside the Rubbing-down House stands well clear, while his companion rubs a twist of straw under the horse's barrel. Nearby, three raffish-looking characters of the Turf called Trotter, Hardy and Thompson are in conversation.

Francis Sartorius Sr (1734–1804): *John Corbet, Robert Leighton and John Kynaston, Members of the Shrewsbury Hunt*, 1779

Francis Sartorius and his son, John Nost, were very popular painters and received a large number of commissions for both racing and hunting subjects. In fact their abilities were strictly limited and there is a repetitiveness about much of their work.

Johann Elias Ridinger
(1698–1767): Two engravings
from *Neue Reit Schul*, Augsburg, 1734.
RIGHT *Passage to the left against
a wall*
FAR RIGHT *Capriole*, one
of the most spectacular school jumps

Haute École, that advanced form
of dressage which allows the
horse to perform difficult
acrobatic feats in an apparently
effortless and rhythmic manner,
grew out of the revival of the art
of equitation which began in
the sixteenth century and
developed, particularly in
France, England and Austria,
in the following centuries.

La Croupe à la mu, Die Crouppe an der Crupina ad parietis raille à gauche. wand lincks. sinistram.

Caprioles par le Capriol gerad Capriolus Droite. aus. rectá.

HON.ble MARCIA PITT.   HON.ble GEORGE PITT.   Thos Gooch 1782

LEFT Thomas Gooch (exhibited 1777–1802):
*The Hon. Marcia and the Hon. George Pitt riding in the Park at Stratfield Saye, Hampshire,*1782
RIGHT George Stubbs: *John and Sophia Musters out riding at Colwick Hall, Nottingham,* 1777

Riding has always been a favourite outdoor pastime for the wealthy and in these two paintings, separated as they are in date by only five years, the sitters are dressed in the height of fashion. Gooch portrays the Hon. George Pitt, son of the first Baron Rivers and later Agasse's patron, at the age of thirty-one, out riding with his sister Marcia in the grounds of Stratfield Saye, an estate in Hampshire. Musters had the figures of himself and his wife painted out of Stubbs's picture, probably because of his wife's infidelity, and had two walking grooms put in by another hand. The painting was restored in 1938.

LEFT Thomas Gooch: *Lord Abergavenny's Dark Bay Carriage Horse waiting with a Terrier outside the Coach-house at Eridge Castle, Sussex*, 1785
RIGHT William Shaw (active 1760–72): *The Duke of Ancaster's Bay Stallion Blank walking towards a Mare*, c. 1770

Throughout the eighteenth and nineteenth centuries, the possession of elegant carriages drawn by fine horses was as important to their owners as driving a prestigious motor car is today. Artists such as Gooch, commissioned to paint these horses and carriages, usually tried to please their patrons by accentuating the smartness of the equipment.

It is interesting to compare Shaw's study of a stallion being led to a mare with the portrait of Bay Ascham by Jacques-Laurent Agasse (p. 120); while the latter is painted in the nineteenth-century idiom, Shaw's handling of the subject looks backwards to James Seymour and Thomas Spencer.

LEFT Sawrey Gilpin, RA (1733–1807):
A Grey Arab Horse, c. 1792
RIGHT Sir Henry Raeburn, RA (1756–1823):
The Painter's son Henry on a Pony, c. 1795

The romantic element in Sawrey Gilpin's picture, with its
stark lighting and tense movement, foreshadows the work of
Géricault. Gilpin's subject matter was usually in a gentler
idiom, and he frequently painted the horses in the landscape
paintings of other artists such as George Barret.

Raeburn's professional career, spanning some thirty years,
was spent as a fashionable portrait painter in Scotland.
The charming picture of his younger son, Henry, astride
his pony was evidently made for his personal pleasure.

The Dray Horse

London Publish'd 15th March 1787

The Road Horse

S. Gilpin

London Publish'd 15th March 1787

The Cart Horse

London Publish'd 15th March 1787

The Coach Horse

London Publish'd 15th March 1787

Sawrey Gilpin:
FAR LEFT ABOVE *The Dray Horse*
FAR LEFT BELOW *The Cart Horse*
LEFT BELOW *The Coach Horse*
LEFT ABOVE *The Road Horse*, 1787

Four etchings from a series of eight, the others being *The Pad*, *The Managed Horse*, *The Hunter* and *The Racehorse*. Series such as these dealing with different types of horse, as well as sets portraying the 'Ages of the Horse' from foal to 'meat for the hounds' and the events of the hunting field, were greatly in demand in this period from sporting painters and engravers.

Duke of Grafton. viewing his Stud

Caricaturists have frequently found that the antics of riders and their mounts provide irresistible material. Bunbury, second son of Sir William Bunbury, was an amateur artist and caricaturist who published his *Academy for Grown Horsemen* in 1787 under the pseudonym 'Geoffrey Gambado'. Rowlandson loved drawing horses, but as in his portrayal of people, character weighed more heavily than breeding.

THE NINETEENTH CENTURY AND THE MODERN WORLD

FAR LEFT Théodore Géricault (1791–1824):
Cavalry Officer on Horseback, 1812
LEFT Théodore Géricault:
Horses held by Slaves
RIGHT Théodore Géricault:
The Derby at Epsom, 1821

Géricault and Delacroix were the leading horse painters in French Romantic art during the early years of the nineteenth century. Later Degas's representations of horses in painting, drawing and sculpture created a revolution in artistic vision.

Géricault, during his early career when he was influenced by the appeal of glory and heroism so prevalent in the years of the Napoleonic Empire, painted a number of military subjects. In his *Cavalry Officer on Horseback* he has adopted the classic movement of the battle piece.

In 1816, after the fall of Napoleon, Géricault made his way to Rome where he witnessed the riderless horse race at the Carnival. The spectacle inspired him to paint a number of pictures relating tensions and movement between horses and man such as *Horses held by Slaves*.

Géricault came to England in 1820 with his masterpiece *The Raft of the Medusa*. During his stay he studied the work of English animal artists and painted his *The Derby at Epsom*. The scene, dramatically enacted against a dark sky, makes most English renderings of the racecourse appear prosaic by comparison.

ABOVE Eugène Delacroix (1798–1863):
Study of a Horse, 26 December 1852
ABOVE RIGHT Jacques-Louis David
(1748–1825): *Study of an Antique Horse*
OPPOSITE Théodore Géricault:
A Grey Stallion, c. 1815

David became the arbiter of Neo-classical
taste in France before and during the
Revolution. His drawing is reminiscent of
the statuette of a rearing horse found at
Herculaneum (p. 47) and may well have
been copied direct from an antique
sculpture. His forceful influence on artistic
circles came to an end with his exile at the
time of the restoration of the monarchy, a
time when Romanticism burst forth in the
work of Géricault and Delacroix. Both the
latter had a pre-disposition for painting
horses and associated them, as perhaps no
other artists have, with unbridled strength
and energy.

LEFT Jacques-Laurent
Agasse (1767–1849):
*Bay Ascham, led through
a Gate to a Mare*, 1802–4

RIGHT Jacques-Laurent
Agasse: *Study of
a Grey Horse, c.* 1800

Agasse was born in
Geneva and studied
under David in Paris
before coming to
England in 1800 where
he painted a number of
horse pictures for Lord
Rivers, including the
portrait of Bay Ascham.
The entries in his *Day
Book* which records his
commissions bear witness
to his commitment to
horse painting, although
he also painted land-
scape and genre subjects.

RIGHT Henry Bernard Chalon (1770–1849): *A Groom with a Bay Hunter in a Park, c.* 1800

Chalon records an unpretentious scene where an elderly groom holds the heavy, weight-carrying hunter while a pet terrier runs past.

carle Vernet.

Carle Vernet (1758–1836):
A Mameluke Archer on Horseback

The Mamelukes were the ruling caste in Egypt at
the time of Napoleon's arrival. They did not
marry but replaced their numbers by purchasing
children from poor peasant families in southern
Russia, and converting them to Islam. Their
profession was warfare and they were highly
accomplished horsemen. They have been
described as 'A band of lawless adventurers, slaves
in origin, butchers by choice, turbulent,
bloodthirsty, and too often treacherous . . .' They
had been in Egypt for five and a half centuries and
had changed little in that time, but all their
ferocity and courage on their horses was no match
for the cannonade of the French artillery and the
concentrated fire from the French squares.
The splendidly dressed Mameluke in Vernet's
drawing is adopting the tactic employed so effectively by the ancient Scythians of shooting arrows
backward over his shoulder while retreating.

ABOVE Théodore Chasseriau (1819–56): *Hadji Barbary Stallion from the Province of Constantine*, 1853
ABOVE RIGHT Carle Vernet: *A Turkish Groom holding an Arab Stallion*

Chasseriau was a Creole-born artist of South American origin who went to Paris and became a pupil of Ingres. He was a talented horse painter as is shown in his portrait of a horse from North Africa.

Vernet painted and drew horses throughout his long career. Most of his work took graphic form, with an element of caricature, but he also met a demand for battle scenes and later, after the Napoleonic Wars, for hunting scenes. In the painting of the rearing Arab stallion he has dressed the groom in suitable oriental garb.

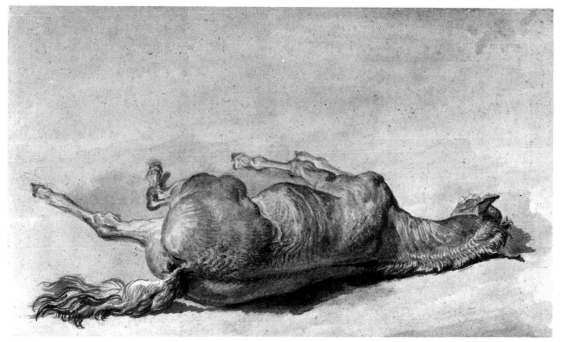

LEFT James Ward, RA (1769–1859):
Colonel Platoff on his Charger
ABOVE James Ward: *A Horse Rolling*
RIGHT James Ward: *A Grey Arabian Stallion, the Property
of Sir Watkin Williams-Wynne, c. 1815–20*

James Ward's true *métier* is evident to posterity, but in his own day he and many
other artists were diverted by the insidious hand of 'refined taste' which pointed
towards history painting as the only truly ennobling subject. Ward spent many
years and disrupted his career by painting an enormous picture commemorating
Wellington's victory at Waterloo. Géricault faced the same dilemma in the
wake of David and French academic painting, but managed to infuse his
romanticism into his great work *The Raft of the Medusa*. Both Géricault and
Ward, however, were at home painting horses, which they loved, and where
their true romantic feelings were able to find their most natural outlet.

LEFT James Ward:
Portrait of Eagle, the Celebrated Stallion, 1809
RIGHT James Ward:
John Levett hunting in the Park at Wychnor, 1817

The extraordinary painting of Eagle, exhibited
at the Royal Academy in 1810, has all the
anatomical understanding of a picture by Stubbs
yet heralds a new age in which the accent on form
characteristic of the classical era is replaced by a
romantic sense of bursting energy and force. Ward
has brilliantly exhibited these qualities in every
muscle and tendon of the horse and he rightly
drew praise from Géricault for his abilities.

Although Ward's skill in painting animals was a
dominant element in his art, his interests were
diverse, too much so to guarantee his success.
A highly skilled engraver, he also had ambitions
as a landscape painter and for the background
of his picture of John Levett he has adopted a
Rubenesque style. The real strength of the picture,
however, lies in the painting of the horse and rider.

LEFT ABOVE John Ferneley Sr (1781–1860):
William Massey-Stanley driving his Cabriolet in Hyde Park, 1833
LEFT BELOW James Pollard (1797–1859):
The Louth–London Royal Mail travelling by Train from Peterborough East, Northamptonshire, 1845?
ABOVE James Pollard: *The Derby Pets: The Arrival*, c. 1842

Transportation in the nineteenth century was much facilitated by improvements to the roads as well as by the skill of coachbuilders. Coaches and their horses were occasionally carried on the rapidly increasing network of railways. Private driving vehicles, stage coaches, and a new feature – travelling horse boxes – were to be seen at this period.

ABOVE John Dalby (active 1840–53):
Fox Hunting: Clearing a Bank, c. 1840
ABOVE RIGHT Edwin Cooper of Beccles
(active *c.* 1820): *A Sportsman with
a Shooting Pony and Gun Dogs*

Fox hunting and field sports generally were pursued with great enthusiasm and dedication in the nineteenth century. They were no longer the private preserve of squires and noblemen but were increasingly enjoyed by members of the middle class. Writers and painters were at hand to meet a steady demand and to record in books and pictures the sportsmen's exploits. The average level of artistic accomplishment was not very high but sometimes, as the paintings by Dalby and Cooper show, minor artists produced work of outstanding merit.

ABOVE John Frederick Herring Sr
(1795–1865): *The Greengrocer's Cob*, 1851
ABOVE RIGHT Anson Ambrose Martin
(English School, 19th century): *James Taylor Wray
of the Bedale Hunt with his Dun Hunter*, 1840

Herring's charming scene, bordering as it does
on sentimentality, was painted for a clientele
who, because of the Industrial Revolution, was
becoming ever further removed from rustic

quietude, and who liked to see on the walls of
their urban or suburban houses pictures which
evoked nostalgia for the simple country life.

The painting of a slightly self-conscious
country gentleman about to mount his hunter
and hack off to the Meet has a particularly
attractive quality. The obscure painter Anson
Martin has clearly taken a great deal of trouble
over his commission, particularly with the
foreshortening of the horse.

John Frederick Herring Sr,
sometimes aided by his three
sons, John Frederick Jr,
Benjamin and Charles, was an
enormously popular painter of
horses in the mid-nineteenth
century. His son's picture may
depict no specific meeting, but
his own canvas shows the start
of what became known as
'the dirtiest Derby in history',
which was saying something
for a period when standards of
conduct on the Turf left much
to be desired. As was often the
case, the cheating involved
much complicated and
devious skullduggery.

LEFT Lady Elizabeth Butler (1846–1933):
'Scotland Forever!' – The Charge of the Scots Greys at Waterloo, 1881
RIGHT Sir Edwin Landseer, RA (1802–73):
The Young Queen Victoria on Horseback, 1838?

Remembered by many from childhood as an engraving hanging on
the back staircases of English country houses, Lady Butler's painting
is the quintessence of High Victorian bombast. As a history picture
it stands no comparison with the work of Meissonier, yet there is a
vulgar bravura about it which perhaps accounted for its popularity.
    Landseer's artistic approach was heavily larded with many of the
sentiments which today we associate with the Victorian age, and
occasionally his work manifested a streak of vicious cruelty. But for
all that he was a very fine animal painter. He has managed perfectly
to convey a sense of movement and poise in his treatment of
the horse in this painting.

LEFT Edward Troye (1808–74):
American Eclipse
ABOVE Edward Troye: *Self-portrait*, 1852
ABOVE RIGHT William S. Mount (1807–68):
Bargaining for a Horse, 1835

Troye is undoubtedly America's foremost nineteenth-century horse painter. Swiss-born, he studied in England for six years before emigrating to the West Indies in 1828. After several years in Jamaica he went to work in the United States, for the most part in Philadelphia, Virginia and the South. The portrait of American Eclipse is typical of his work. The horse was named after, but was no relation to, Eclipse, the greatest English racehorse of the eighteenth century. American Eclipse gave his breeder such an impression of speed and energy when he was only five months old that he was considered worthy to bear the name. He proved to be almost invincible on the race course.

Mount's narrative scene is filled with anecdotal material of which the horse is only a part.

ABOVE George Catlin (1794–1872)
A Crow Chief on Horseback in rich Costume, 1832
ABOVE RIGHT Frederic Remington (1861–1909): *The Cheyenne Buck*, 1901
LEFT Alfred Jacob Miller (1810–74): *Snake Indians*

Catlin acquired an intimate knowledge of the Plains Indians from living with them and painting them in the 1830s and '40s. Although some of his 'primitive' pictures show their bloodthirsty ways, others reflect the artist's ready sense of humour. In the painting of a Crow Chief the horse emulates his rider's ferocious expression – and his headgear. Remington presents a more realistic view of the Indian and his horse at the turn of the century, while Miller, a Baltimore artist, portrays a rather romantic image of Indian scouts surveying their territory. The Indians obtained their horses by stealing them from the white man or by capturing the prairie Mustangs.

ABOVE Jean-Louis-Ernest Meissonier (1815–91):
Sketch for a Figure in a Tricorn Hat on Horseback, c. 1879–85
ABOVE RIGHT Briton Riviere, RA (1840–1920):
In Manus Tuas Domine, 1879
OPPOSITE Jean-Louis-Ernest Meissonier:
Campagne de France, 1814, 1861

There was a strong vogue for paintings of military subjects in mid-century France and Meissonier filled this demand with period scenes painted in the salon tradition. His carefully executed pictures were based on a very thorough knowledge of draughtsmanship.

Like many nineteenth-century genre painters who introduced animals into their work, Riviere has tended to endow his horse and hounds with human qualities and attitudes.

LEFT René Princeteau
(1844–1914):
Chevaux de Course sur la Plage
RIGHT Alfred de Dreux
(1810–60):
Retour de la Course

The relatively rapid rise and
spread of horse racing in nineteenth-century France resulted
in its being frequently used as
subject-matter by French artists
who explored the theme in many
different ways. Princeteau's scene
of lads exercising racehorses on
the beach reveals his use of strong
colour and free brush-work.

In De Dreux's enchanting and
mildly humorous painting,
a rugged-up racehorse and a
hack are being led by a man
who strides out for home
into a biting wind after an
obviously unsuccessful day.
Even the dog which accompanies
them seems to share in their
sense of disappointment.

LEFT Jean-Louis Forain (1852–1931):
Les Courses à Deauville
ABOVE James McNeill Whistler
(1834–1903): *The Good Shoe*, 1895

Forain's fine draughtsmanship with its never
absent note of caricature, perfectly captures
the flavour of French racecourse scenes of the
period. Whistler's glimpse into a farrier's shop
comes from his 'London and Paris' scenes.

ABOVE Eugène Louis Lami (1800–90): *Groom à Cheval*, 1836
RIGHT Pierre Auguste Renoir (1841–1919): *Riding in
the Bois de Boulogne*, 1873

Lami's intimate watercolour drawing is by another artist who, like Whistler,
was equally at home in France and England. Renoir, an artist who was
not accustomed to painting horses, has nevertheless produced an elegant
picture of a lady riding side-saddle accompanied by a boy. Around 1900,
with the growth of feminism and an increasing participation by women in
sport, women began to abandon the side-saddle and to ride astride.

LEFT Edgar Degas (1834–1917): *Studies of Horses*, 1866–72?
ABOVE Edgar Degas: *Chevaux dans la Prairie*, 1871

The advent of photography not only revealed the true movements of the horse but also enabled artists to look at compositions with the sharp-edged eye of the camera. Painters like Degas, Bonnard and Vuillard, while retaining their artistic licence, used this factor to their advantage. In Degas's relatively early pencil studies of horses his mastery of line is already apparent.

Edgar Degas:
Thirteen Statuettes of Horses

A beautiful and unique collection of waxes made by constructing armatures and then pressing soft, high-temperature melting wax onto them. The waxes were then used to make casts, and bronzes were taken from the casts by the traditional method. In this way Degas captured movement in his studies of horses and ballet dancers. Many of Degas's paintings and sculptures of horses in motion are directly based on Eadweard Muybridge's photographs in *Animal Locomotion*.

LEFT Edgar Degas: *Les Cavaliers, c.* 1885
ABOVE Edgar Degas: *Horse with Jockey up, c.* 1889
RIGHT Edgar Degas: *Jockeys in the Rain, c.* 1886?

Although there is no proof that Degas was an
enthusiastic racegoer, nevertheless he found in horses
the perfect subject with which to express his feeling for
movement and form. Constantly exploring the effects
of light and viewpoint, he invested in his subjects
an abundance of energy.

LEFT Henri de Toulouse-Lautrec (1864–1901): *Le Tandem*, 1899
ABOVE Constantin Guys (1802–92): *Militaires en Parade*

The circus scene was drawn at the very end of Toulouse-Lautrec's brief life.
Born into an aristocratic family, he suffered a riding accident when he was a
child in which his legs were crippled with the result that he was effectively
dwarfed. During convalescence he turned to drawing and, despite his
misfortune, featured horses extensively in his brilliant illustrations.

Guys's work is prolific, the result of a desperate struggle to make a living.
In consequence his drawings are uneven in quality, but his illustrations,
including many of horse-drawn carriages and military subjects, exhibit
a sound understanding of horse draughtsmanship.

ABOVE Pierre Bonnard (1867–1947): *Horse's Head*, *c.* 1906
RIGHT Odilon Redon (1840–1916): *Pegasus*, *c.* 1895

Bonnard's drawing is a reminder of the days when the horse's useful function in society was first superseded by mechanized transport. The illustration, portraying a horse's frightened reaction to the unexpected, comes from a unique collection of 104 Chinese ink drawings by Bonnard which illustrated *La 628–E8*, an imaginative account by Octave Mirbeau of a series of motorcar journeys through France, Belgium, Holland and Germany between 1905 and 1907. The weak anatomy of the horse in Odilon Redon's print is redeemed by its dream-like quality.

LEFT Paul Gauguin (1848–1903): *The White Horse*, 1898
ABOVE Pablo Picasso (1881–1973): *The Horse*, 1901

Gauguin has portrayed the horse in his painting, not as a symbol of strength and nobility, but as part of a scene of primitive idyllic beauty. It stands in a shimmering pool of water, while in the background natives are seated bareback astride their small horses, bathed in a warm dappled light.

The little sketch by Picasso, made in Barcelona shortly after his first visit to Paris, at the commencement of his Blue Period, reveals the twenty-year-old artist's extraordinary talent and absolute grasp of draughtsmanship.

LEFT Pablo Picasso:
Harlequin on Horseback, 1904
ABOVE Franz Marc (1880–1916):
The Yellow Horses, 1910–11

When Picasso first visited Paris in 1900, he was strongly attracted to the work of Toulouse-Lautrec and Forain, both brilliant at drawing horses. His reflective study of *Harlequin on Horse-back* dates from the beginning of his Circus Period.

Marc's work, and that of his fellow artists in the Blaue Reiter group, was a reaction to the complexities of modern society; he sought instead a more primitive form of artistic expression. His deep love of horses was expressed in many paintings which used them as subject matter, among them *The Yellow Horses* – a picture which has a spiritual affinity with Gauguin's *The White Horse*. Marc's career ended abruptly when he perished at the front during the First World War.

LEFT Robert Polhill Bevan (1865–1925): *The Cab Horse*, 1910
ABOVE Jack Butler Yeats (1871–1957): *The Squireen*, 1899

As the horse lost its essential role in society so it lost much of its
grandeur too. These two paintings depict the horse as a very ordinary
animal with no romantic or heroic associations. Bevan, in his
paintings of cabs and horse sales, was one of the very few artists of
note to portray the horses which were present in London in such large
numbers during the early years of the present century.

Ben Nicholson (b.1894): *Rambler 2*, 1977

The principle of a subtle suggestion of
recession, obtained in Nicholson's earlier
work through the relationships of straight
lines and circles, sometimes with the
introduction of low relief, is pursued in
Rambler 2 by the insertion into the
composition of a primitively drawn horse
contained within a separate loose
framework on a linear flat landscape.

ABOVE George Bellows (1882–1925):
Polo at Lakewood, 1910
ABOVE RIGHT Sir Alfred Munnings, PRA
(1878–1959): *After the Race ; Cheltenham
Saddling Paddock, c.* 1937
OPPOSITE Sir Alfred Munnings:
*Royal Minstrel, owned by John Hay Whitney
with Joe Childs up,* 1929

In the twentieth century traditional
representations of the horse have
continued to be popular alongside more
innovatory and experimental
approaches to the subject. Bellows's
lively picture attempts to depict
movement and tension in the ponies
with much the same spirit as appears in
the work of Géricault and Degas.

Munnings's extrovert bohemian attitudes
disguised a strictly conventional approach
towards painting. However, he built on
a sound knowledge of horse anatomy to
combine a panache and sureness of touch
with an extraordinary ability to capture
the atmosphere of the racecourse.

List of Illustrations

1 William Blake (1757–1827): *The Horse*, *c.* 1805, pen and tempera on gesso primed copper plate, $4\frac{1}{2} \times 2\frac{3}{4}$ in. From the Collection of Mr and Mrs Paul Mellon, Upperville, Virginia

6 George Stubbs, ARA (1724–1806): *Pumpkin with a Stable-lad*, 1774, oil on canvas, $31\frac{1}{2} \times 39\frac{1}{2}$ in. From the Collection of Mr and Mrs Paul Mellon, Upperville, Virginia

10 The White Horse near Uffington, Berkshire, England, 1st century AD, chalk hill figure, length 374 ft. (Photo: The National Trust)

11 Model of a Scythian archer or possibly an Amazon, Etruscan, *c.*500 BC, cast bronze, length $5\frac{7}{8}$ in. The British Museum, London

12 Detail of a chariot race from a Greek vase, 490–80 BC, clay. The British Museum, London

13 James Seymour (1702–52): detail of *The Chaise Match run on Newmarket Heath on Wednesday, 29 August 1750*, oil on canvas, 42×66 in. From the Collection of Mr and Mrs Paul Mellon, Upperville, Virginia

14 David Dalby of York (1790–1840): *Signal, a Grey Arab, with a Groom in the Desert*, 1829, oil on canvas, $23\frac{1}{2} \times 29\frac{1}{2}$ in. From the Collection of Mr and Mrs Paul Mellon, Upperville, Virginia

15 *Grooming a Stallion*, Safawid Persia, late 16th century AD, miniature, $7\frac{7}{8} \times 11\frac{7}{8}$ in. The British Museum, London

16 Antonio Pisanello (1395–1455): *Study of the Neck and Head of a bridled Horse seen face on*, *c.* 1430–40, pen and pencil, $10\frac{5}{8} \times 6\frac{5}{8}$ in. Musée du Louvre, Paris

Théodore Géricault (1791–1824): *Head of a White Horse*, 1810–12, oil on canvas, $25\frac{5}{8} \times 21\frac{1}{4}$ in. Musée du Louvre, Paris

17 George Stubbs, ARA, (1724–1806): finished study for the second of the three skeleton tables and finished study for the eighth of the fifteen anatomical tables in *The Anatomy of the Horse* (1766), 1758–9, pencil, $14 \times 7\frac{3}{4}$ in. The Royal Academy, London

18 Benjamin Herring (d. 1871): *The Start of the Race for the Cambridgeshire Stakes, Newmarket, Tuesday, 22 October 1867*, oil on canvas, $29\frac{3}{4} \times 57\frac{1}{2}$ in. From the Collection of Mr and Mrs Paul Mellon, Upperville, Virginia

19 Edouard Manet (1832–1883): *The Races at Longchamp*, 1864, oil on canvas, $17\frac{1}{4} \times 33\frac{1}{4}$ in. Collection of the Art Institute of Chicago (Potter Palmer Collection), Chicago

20 Cave painting from Lascaux, France, *c.* 10,000 BC, earth colours on rock. (Photo: Hans Hinz, Basle)

21 Belt plaque, Sakic culture, 4th century BC, gold, $6 \times 5\frac{3}{4}$ in. The Hermitage, Leningrad (Photo: Novosti Press)

Detail of the Great Vessel from the Tomb of the Princess at Vix, Châtillon-sur-Seine, Greek-Italian origin, 5th century BC, bronze, height $64\frac{1}{2}$ in. (Photo: The Rev. R. V. Schoder, Loyola University, Chicago)

24 Detail from the west frieze of the interior colonnade of the Parthenon, Greek, 5th century BC, marble relief. The British Museum, London

25 Head and forepart of one of the four horses originally surmounting the Mausoleum at Halicarnassus, Greek, *c.* 350 BC, marble, height 7 ft. 10 in. The British Museum, London

26 *The Flying Horse standing on one leg on a Swallow*, Chinese, Eastern Han Dynasty (AD 25–222), bronze, length $17\frac{3}{4}$ in., height $9\frac{5}{8}$ in. Shensi Provincial Museum, Sian, China (Photo: Robert Harding Associates)

27 Albrecht Dürer (1471–1528): *The Knight, Death and the Devil*, 1513, engraving, $9\frac{5}{8} \times 7\frac{1}{2}$ in. The British Museum, London

Detail of *The Triumph of an Emperor* (possibly Anastasius I) known as *The Barberini Ivory*, Constantinople, *c.* AD 500, ivory, $13\frac{3}{8} \times 10\frac{5}{8}$ in. Musée du Louvre, Paris

29 *Equestrian Statue of Marcus Aurelius*, Roman, 2nd century AD, bronze. Piazza del Campidoglio, Rome (Photo: Scala)

31 Paolo Uccello (1396/7–1475): *The Hunt*, after 1460, $25\frac{5}{8} \times 65$ in. The Ashmolean Museum, Oxford

33 Titian (1488/90–1576): *The Emperor Charles V before the Battle of Mühlberg*, 1548, oil on canvas, $130\frac{3}{4} \times 109\frac{7}{8}$ in. Museo del Prado, Madrid

36 George Stubbs, ARA (1724–1806): *Whistlejacket*, 1761–2, oil on canvas, 128×102 in. Collection: Earl Fitzwilliam, Kenwood House, London (Photo: Cooper-Bridgeman Library)

37 Jacques-Louis David (1748–1825): *Bonaparte crossing the Alps*, 1800, oil on canvas, $111\frac{3}{8} \times 79\frac{1}{2}$ in. Musée de Malmaison, Paris (Photo: Giraudon)

40 Edgar Degas (1834–1917): *Steeplechase . . . The Fallen Jockey*, 1866, oil on canvas, $71 \times 59\frac{1}{2}$ in. From the Collection of Mr and Mrs Paul Mellon, Upperville, Virginia

41 Marino Marini (b. 1901): *Horse*, bronze, height $30\frac{1}{2}$ in. The National Gallery of Canada, Ottawa

42 *Pharaoh Seti I in a war Chariot*; detail of a stone carving from the temple of Amun at Karnak, Egyptian, 1st millennium BC, sandstone.

Archer and Charioteer; bas-relief from Carchemish in Northern Syria, Neo-Hittite, 9th century BC, stone. The Hittite Museum, Ankara

43 *King Tiglath-pileser III standing in his Chariot under a Parasol*; bas-relief from the palace of Nimrud, Assyrian, 8th century BC, gypsum, $74 \times 76\frac{3}{4}$ in. The British Museum, London

44 *Horse on a Stand*, Greek, 570–700 BC, bronze, height $3\frac{1}{2}$ in. The British Museum, London

Horse and Rider, Greek, *c.* 500 BC, terracotta, height 2 in. The British Museum, London

Mounted Cavalryman, Greek, *c.*550 BC, bronze, height 10 in. The British Museum, London

45 Helmet, Greek *c.* 600 BC, bronze, height $9\frac{5}{8}$ in. The Norbert Schimmel Collection, New York

46 Head of a horse from the chariot of Selene, from the east pediment of the Parthenon, Greek, 5th century BC, marble, length $32\frac{5}{8}$ in. The British Museum, London

47 Detail of a battle scene from the *Alexander Sarcophagus*, Greek, 4th century BC. The Archaeological Museum, Istanbul

A Rearing Horse, South Italy, *c.* AD 50, bronze. Museo Nazionale, Naples (Photo: The Mansell Collection)

48 Detail of a horse from St Mark's Cathedral, Venice, Roman, *c.* 400–200 BC, bronze, $92\frac{1}{2} \times 98\frac{3}{4}$ in. (Photo: A. F. Kersting)

Amazons on Horseback, Etruscan, late 6th century BC, silver panel with gold sections, diameter $7\frac{3}{4}$ in. The British Museum, London

49 *A Vandal Landowner*, North Africa, *c.* AD 500, mosaic, $66\frac{1}{2} \times 96\frac{1}{2}$ in. The British Museum, London

A four-horse Chariot approaching the Goals, Roman, 1st century AD, terracotta, $12 \times 16\frac{1}{4}$ in. The British Museum, London

A two-horse Chariot, Roman, 1st–2nd century AD, bronze, $7\frac{3}{4} \times 10$ in. The British Museum, London

50 *Head of a Horse*, Chinese, 6 Dynasties (AD 222–589), terracotta, length $8\frac{1}{2}$ in. Collection: King Gustaf of Sweden

51 *Horse*, Chinese, 6 Dynasties (AD 222–589), terracotta, height $11\frac{1}{4}$ in. Reitberg Museum, Zurich

Horse, Chinese, late 6th–early 8th century AD, painted stucco, height $23\frac{1}{2}$ in. The British Museum, London

Equestrian Figure, Chinese, T'ang Dynasty (AD 618–906), terracotta, height 23 in. The St Louis Art Museum, St Louis, Missouri

52 *Horses with Grooms*, Chinese, T'ang Dynasty (AD 618–906) glazed pottery, height of horses 32 in. and $23\frac{5}{8}$ in. The British Museum, London

53 Horse's head in the form of a rhyton, Persian, Sassanian Dynasty (AD 224–642), silver, length $10\frac{5}{8}$ in. The Cincinnati Art Museum, Cincinnati, Ohio

54 Detail of Norman cavalry from *The Bayeux Tapestry*, 11th century, woollen embroidery, height 20 in. Musée de la Reine Mathilde, Bayeux

55 Giovanni di Paolo (*c.* 1403–*c.* 1482): *The Triumph of Death*, 1450–60?, miniature, leaf size $24\frac{7}{8} \times 15\frac{3}{4}$ in. Biblioteca Comunale, Siena (Photo: Scala)

The Master of the Housebook (active 1465–1500): *Wild Men Jousting*, engraving, $4\frac{7}{8} \times 7\frac{1}{2}$ in. The Rijksmuseum, Amsterdam

The Lion and the Horse; an illustration from Aesop's *Leben und Fabeln*, Augsburg, 1479, woodcut. The Metropolitan Museum of Art (The Harris Brisbane Dick Fund, 1937), New York

56 Simone Martini (1284–1344): *Guidoriccio da Fogliano on Horseback*, 1328, fresco, 11 ft. 1 in. × 31 ft. 7 in. Palazzo Pubblico, Siena (Photo: Scala)

57 Italian School: *Tournament Scene*, *c.* 1460, drawing, $11\frac{7}{8} \times 16\frac{1}{2}$ in. The British Museum, London

58 Lucas Cranach the Elder (1472–1553): *St George on Horseback with the dead Dragon*, 1507, woodcut in gold on blue tinted paper, $9\frac{3}{8} \times 6\frac{1}{4}$ in. The British Museum, London

Hans Burgkmair (1473–1559): *The Emperor Maximilian I on Horseback*, 1508, woodcut in gold on crimson red paper, $13\frac{3}{4} \times 9\frac{1}{2}$ in. The Ashmolean Museum, Oxford

59 Benozzo Gozzoli (1420–97): *The Journey of the Magi to Bethlehem*, 1463, fresco, 12 ft. 6 in. × 16 ft. 9 in. Palazzo Medici-Riccardi, Florence (Photo: Scala)

60 Antonio Pisanello (1395–1455): *The Vision of St Eustace*, 1436–8, oil on canvas, $21\frac{1}{2} \times 25\frac{3}{4}$ in. The National Gallery, London

61 Albrecht Dürer (1471–1528): *The Vision of St Eustace*, *c.* 1501, engraving, $10\frac{1}{8} \times 10\frac{1}{4}$ in. The British Museum, London

62 René d'Anjou (1409–80): *Tournament Ceremonial* from *Traité de la Forme et Devis d'un Tournois*, illumination. Bibliothèque Nationale, Paris

63 The Limbourg brothers (active first half of the 15th century): *August* from *Les Très Riches Heures du Duc de Berry*, miniature illumination, $8\frac{1}{2} \times 5\frac{1}{2}$ in. Musée Condé, Chantilly (Photo: Giraudon)

Ploughing Scene, Flemish, 1416, miniature illumination, $4\frac{1}{2} \times 3\frac{1}{4}$ in. The British Museum, London

64 Paolo Uccello (1396/7–1475): *Monument to Sir John Hawkwood*, 1425–36, fresco, 26 ft. 11 in. × 16 ft. 10 in. Basilica di S. Maria del Fiore, Florence (Photo: Scala)

Paolo Uccello: *St George and the Dragon*, *c.* 1455, oil on canvas, $22\frac{1}{4} \times 29\frac{1}{4}$ in. The National Gallery, London

65 Paolo Uccello (1396/7–1475): *The Battle of San Romano*, 1435–50, oil on wood, $91\frac{1}{2} \times 130$ in. The National Gallery, London

66 Donatello (*c.* 1386–1466): *The Gattamelata Monument*, 1443–53, bronze, height (without base) $133\frac{7}{8}$ in. The Piazza del Santo, Padua (Photo: Alinari)

Antonio Pollaiuolo (1433–98): *Study for an Equestrian Monument to Francesco Sforza*, *c.* 1490, pen and brown ink with light brown wash on paper, $11\frac{1}{4} \times 9\frac{5}{8}$ in. The Metropolitan Museum of Art (Lehman Collection), New York

67 Leonardo da Vinci (1452–1519): *Studies for the Trivulzio Monument*, 1508–11, pen and ink, $11 \times 7\frac{3}{4}$ in. The Royal Library, Windsor (Copyright Reserved)

68 Michelangelo (1475–1564): *Studies of a Horse, and a Horseman attacking Foot Soldiers*, *c.* 1505, pen and brown ink, $16\frac{3}{4} \times 11\frac{1}{8}$ in. The Ashmolean Museum, Oxford

Antonio Pisanello (1395–1455): *Two Horses*, *c.* 1436–8, pen and pencil, $9\frac{7}{8} \times 6\frac{1}{2}$ in. Musée du Louvre, Paris

69 Albrecht Dürer (1471–1528): *St George*, 1508, engraving, $4\frac{1}{4} \times 3\frac{1}{4}$ in. The British Museum, London

Albrecht Dürer: *Soldier on Horseback with a Lance*, 1498, watercolour, $16\frac{1}{8} \times 13$ in. Graphische Sammlung Albertina, Vienna

70 Lambert Doomer (1623–1700): *Two Farm Horses*, pen and ink, $4 \times 4\frac{7}{8}$ in. The Pushkin Museum, Moscow

Attributed to Roelant Savery (1576–1639): *A Two-horse Team*, 1559–63, pen and brown ink over black chalk, $6\frac{1}{2} \times 7\frac{1}{4}$ in. Graphische Sammlung Albertina, Vienna

71 Hans Baldung Grien (1484/5–1545): *A Stallion in a Herd of Wild Horses*, 1534, woodcut, $8\frac{1}{2} \times 12\frac{1}{2}$ in. The Metropolitan Museum of Art (The Harris Brisbane Dick Fund, 1933), New York

Piero di Cosimo (1462–1521): *Allegory*, *c.* 1500, oil on wood, $22\frac{1}{8} \times 17\frac{3}{8}$ in. The National Gallery of Art (Samuel H. Kress Collection, 1939), Washington DC

72 Raphael (1483–1520): *St George and the Dragon*, 1504–5, oil on panel, $11\frac{1}{4} \times 8\frac{3}{4}$ in. The National Gallery of Art (Andrew C. Mellon Collection), Washington DC

Raphael: *Head of a Horse*, *c.* 1511, black chalk on yellowish-brown paper, $26\frac{3}{4} \times 21$ in. The Ashmolean Museum, Oxford

73 Rinaldo Montovano and Benedetto Pagni (pupils of Giulio Romano, *c.* 1499–1546): detail of fresco decorations in the Sala dei Cavalli, 1527–8. Palazzo del Té, Mantua (Photo: Scala)

Giovanni Bologna or Giambologna (1529–1608): *Horse Prancing*, 1581, bronze, height $9\frac{1}{4}$ in. The Victoria and Albert Museum (Crown Copyright), London

74 El Greco (1540/50–1614): *St Martin and the Beggar*, 1604–14, oil on canvas, $76\frac{1}{4} \times 40\frac{1}{2}$ in. The National Gallery of Art (Widener Collection, 1942), Washington DC

Caravaggio (*c.* 1562–1609): *The Conversion of St Paul*, 1600–1, oil on canvas, $100\frac{1}{2} \times 68\frac{7}{8}$ in. S. Maria del Popolo, Rome (Photo: Alinari)

75 Titian (1488/90–1576): *A Horse and Rider falling*, black chalk on paper, $10\frac{3}{4} \times 10\frac{1}{4}$ in. The Ashmolean Museum, Oxford

Lelio Orsi (1511–87): *A Man holding a rearing Horse*, pen and ink, $8\frac{7}{8} \times 7$ in. The British Museum, London

76 Charles le Brun (1619–90): *The Chancellor Siguier*, 1660, oil on canvas, $116\frac{1}{8} \times 138\frac{1}{8}$ in. Musée du Louvre, Paris

77 Sir Anthony van Dyck (1599–1641): *Charles I on Horseback*, late 1630s, oil on canvas, $144\frac{1}{2} \times 115$ in. The National Gallery, London

Diego Velasquez (1599–1660): *Prince Baltasar Carlos*, 1635–6, oil on canvas, $68\frac{1}{8} \times 82\frac{1}{4}$ in. Museo del Prado, Madrid

78 Sir Anthony van Dyck (1599–1641): *Charles I on Horseback with M. de St Antoine*, 1633, oil on canvas, $145 \times 160\frac{1}{4}$ in. Copyright Reserved

Sir Peter Paul Rubens (1577–1640): *A Knight of the Golden Fleece*, *c.* 1610, oil on canvas, $120 \times 85\frac{1}{4}$ in. Copyright Reserved

79 Sir Peter Paul Rubens (1577–1640): copy after *The Battle of Anghiari*, *c.* 1600–8, pen and black ink with grey and white wash, $19\frac{1}{8} \times 24\frac{3}{4}$ in. Musée du Louvre, Paris

80 Stefano della Bella (1610–64): *Stag Hunt*, pen and brown ink over black chalk, $5\frac{1}{4} \times 9\frac{1}{8}$ in. The Pierpont Morgan Library, New York

81 John Vanderbank (1696–1739): *A Man on Horseback*, 1728, grey wash over pencil, $9\frac{1}{2} \times 6\frac{5}{8}$ in. Henry E. Huntington Library and Art Gallery, San Marino, California

Adrien van der Venne (1589–1662): *A Man on Horseback*, *c.* 1625?, pen and brush in black ink on vellum, $9\frac{1}{4} \times 4\frac{3}{4}$ in. Fondation Dustodia (Collection: F. Lugt), Institut Neerlandais, Paris

82 Aelbert Cuyp (1620–91): *Lady and Gentleman on Horseback*, *c.* 1660, oil on canvas, $48\frac{1}{2} \times 67\frac{3}{4}$ in. The National Gallery of Art (Widener Collection), Washington DC

Philips Wouwermans (1619–68): *The Grey*, oil on canvas, $17\frac{1}{8} \times 15$ in. The Rijksmuseum, Amsterdam

83 Rembrandt van Rijn (1606–69): *The Polish Rider*, 1655, oil on canvas, $45\frac{1}{4} \times 52\frac{1}{2}$ in. Copyright: The Frick Collection, New York

84 Detail of *The Samurai Captain Kumagai Naozane pursuing his Enemy during the Battle of Ichinotani, 1184*, 17th century, Japanese screen painting (Photo: Ivan Morris)

Mongol mounted Archer, Chinese, Ming Dynasty (1386–1644), ink and colour drawing, $22 \times 23\frac{3}{8}$ in. The Victoria and Albert Museum (Crown Copyright), London

85 *A Stallion being Shod*, *c.* 1600, India, Mughal School, tinted drawing on paper, $4\frac{7}{8} \times 6$ in. The British Museum, London

Hawking, *c.* 1725, India, Mughal School, miniature painting, $9\frac{3}{8} \times 4\frac{1}{8}$ in. Reproduced by permission of the Syndics of the Fitzwilliam Museum, Cambridge

86 *The Combat between Rustam and Isfandiar*, Persian School, 14th century, miniature painting, $6\frac{3}{8} \times 11\frac{3}{8}$ in. (full leaf, $15\frac{3}{4} \times 11\frac{1}{2}$ in.). Nelson Gallery-Atkins Museum (Nelson Fund), Kansas City, Missouri

87 *A Horse rising to its Feet*, Chinese, K'ang-Hsi Dynasty (1662–1722), glazed earthenware, length $5\frac{1}{4}$ in. The British Museum, London

A Prince receiving Water at a Well, *c.* 1700, India, Mughal School, miniature painting, $9\frac{3}{4} \times 10\frac{7}{8}$ in. (full leaf, $18\frac{7}{8} \times 12\frac{3}{4}$ in.) Private Collection, London (Photo: Courtesy of Colnaghi, London)

88 James Seymour (1702–52): *Flying Childers galloping to the Left, bridled but not saddled*, *c.* 1793, black chalk, $7\frac{1}{4} \times 10\frac{1}{2}$ in. From the Collection of Mr and Mrs Paul Mellon, Upperville, Virginia

89 James Seymour (1702–52): *Flying Childers with Jockey up*, 1740, oil on canvas, 35×53 in. Courtesy of Christie's, London (Photo: Cooper-Bridgeman Library)

90 James Seymour (1702–52): *The Kill at Ashdown Park*, 1743, oil on canvas, 71×94 in. The Tate Gallery, London

91 Pieter Tillemans (1684–1734): *View of the Round Course at Newmarket, with Racehorses going to the Start for the King's Plate*, *c.* 1720, oil on canvas, $34\frac{1}{2} \times 39\frac{1}{4}$ in. From the Collection of Mr and Mrs Paul Mellon, Upperville, Virginia

92 James Seymour (1702–52): *Sir Rober Burgoyne upon his favourite Horse Badger, with his Bitch Juno*, 1740, oil on canvas, $48\frac{3}{4} \times 69$ in. From the Collection of Mr and Mrs Paul Mellon, Upperville, Virginia

93 James Seymour (1702–52): *Two Horses and a Groom in a Stable*, 1747, oil on canvas, $24\frac{1}{2} \times 29\frac{3}{4}$ in. From the Collection of Mr and Mrs Paul Mellon, Upperville, Virginia

John Wootton (1683?–1764): *Two Stallions Fighting*, c. 1736, oil on canvas, 102×144 in. Collection: Lord Bath, Longleat House, Wiltshire

94 George Stubbs, ARA (1724–1806): *Hambletonian being rubbed down with a Trainer and a Stable-lad*, 1799, oil on canvas, $82\frac{1}{2} \times 144\frac{1}{2}$ in. Mount Stewart, Northern Ireland (Photo: The National Trust)

95 George Stubbs, ARA (1724–1806): *Gimcrack on Newmarket Heath with a Trainer, Jockey and Stable-lad*, 1765, oil on canvas, 40×76 in. Reproduced by kind permission of the Steward of the Jockey Club

96 George Stubbs, ARA (1724–1806): *Racehorses belonging to the Duke of Richmond exercising at Goodwood*, 1760–1, oil on canvas, $50\frac{1}{4} \times 80\frac{3}{4}$ in. From Goodwood House by courtesy of the Trustees (Photo: Cooper-Bridgeman Library)

97 Thomas Sandby, RA (1723–98): *The New North Face of Great Lodge*, c. 1760, pencil, pen and watercolour, $18\frac{3}{4} \times 35\frac{1}{2}$ in. The Royal Library, Windsor (Copyright Reserved)

98 George Stubbs, ARA (1724–1806): *Portrait of a Racehorse: Otho with Jockey up*, 1766, oil on canvas, 40×50 in. The Tate Gallery, London (Gift of Mr Paul Mellon)

99 George Stubbs, ARA (1724–1806): *Portrait of a Racehorse: Turf with Jockey up*, c. 1765, oil on canvas, $40\frac{1}{4} \times 50\frac{1}{4}$ in. Yale Center for British Art (Paul Mellon Collection), New Haven, Connecticut

100–1 George Stubbs, ARA (1724–1806): detail of *Mares and Foals without a Background*, 1762, oil on canvas, 40×75 in. Collection Earl Fitzwilliam (Photo: Cooper-Bridgeman Library)

102 George Stubbs, ARA (1724–1806): *The Prince of Wales's Phaeton*, 1793, oil on canvas, $40\frac{1}{4} \times 50\frac{1}{2}$ in. Copyright Reserved (Photo: A. C. Cooper)

George Stubbs: *Soldiers of the 10th Light Dragoons*, 1793, oil on canvas, 40×50 in. Copyright Reserved (Photo: A. C. Cooper)

103 George Stubbs, ARA (1724–1806): *Flayed Horse*, 1758–9, pencil, $14\frac{1}{2} \times 19\frac{3}{4}$ in.

The Royal Academy, London

George Stubbs: *Portrait of the Racehorse Rufus*, 1762–7, oil on canvas, $23\frac{1}{2} \times 30\frac{1}{2}$ in. Indianapolis Museum of Art, Indianapolis, Indiana

104 George Stubbs, ARA (1724–1806): *Horse attacked by a Lion*, 1769, enamel on copper, $9\frac{1}{2} \times 11\frac{1}{8}$ in. The Tate Gallery, London (Photo: John Webb)

105 George Stubbs, ARA (1724–1806): *Horse frightened by a Lion*, 1770, oil on canvas, 40×50 in. The Walker Art Gallery, Liverpool

106 Ben Marshall (1767–1835): *Muly Moloch, a Chestnut Colt being rubbed down on Newmarket Heath*, 1803, oil on canvas, 40×50 in. From the Collection of Mr and Mrs Paul Mellon, Upperville, Virginia

Francis Sartorius Sr (1734–1804): *John Corbet, Robert Leighton and John Kynaston, Members of the Shrewsbury Hunt*, 1779, oil on canvas, $37\frac{3}{4} \times 57\frac{1}{2}$ in. Yale Center for British Art (Paul Mellon Collection), New Haven, Connecticut

107 Johann Elias Ridinger (1698–1767): *Passage to the left* and *Capriole*; two engravings from *Neue Reit Schul*, Augsburg, 1734, $18\frac{5}{8} \times 14\frac{1}{2}$ in. Private Collection, London (Photo: Angelo Hornak)

108 Thomas Gooch (exhibited 1777–1802): *The Hon. Marcia and the Hon. George Pitt riding in the Park at Stratfield Saye, Hampshire*, 1782, oil on canvas, 27×25 in. From the Collection of Mr and Mrs Paul Mellon, Upperville, Virginia

109 George Stubbs, ARA (1724–1806): *John and Sophia Musters out riding at Colwick Hall, Nottingham*, 1777, oil on canvas, $38 \times 50\frac{1}{2}$ in. Collection: Major Musters, Nottingham (Photo: Cooper-Bridgeman Library)

110 Thomas Gooch (exhibited 1777–1802): *Lord Abergavenny's Dark Bay Carriage Horse waiting with a Terrier outside the Coach-house at Eridge Castle, Sussex*, 1785, oil on canvas, $24\frac{1}{2} \times 29\frac{1}{4}$ in. From the Collection of Mr and Mrs Paul Mellon, Upperville, Virginia

111 William Shaw (active 1760–72): *The Duke of Ancaster's Bay Stallion Blank walking towards a Mare*, c. 1770, oil on canvas, $40\frac{1}{4} \times 50\frac{1}{4}$ in. From the Collection of Mr and Mrs Paul Mellon, Upperville, Virginia

112 Sawrey Gilpin, RA (1733–1807): *A Grey Arab Horse*, c. 1792, oil on canvas, 28×36 in. Reproduced by permission of the Syndics of the Fitzwilliam Museum, Cambridge

113 Sir Henry Raeburn, RA (1756–1823): *The Painter's son Henry on a Pony*, c. 1795, oil on canvas, $13\frac{7}{8} \times 9\frac{1}{4}$ in. The National Gallery of Scotland, Edinburgh (Photo: Tom Scott)

114 Sawrey Gilpin, RA (1733–1807): *The Dray Horse*; *The Cart Horse*; *The Coach Horse*; *The Road Horse*, 1787, etchings, each $5\frac{1}{2} \times 7\frac{3}{4}$ in. Private Collection, London

115 Henry Bunbury (1750–1811): *How to ride genteel and agreeable down hill* from *An Academy for Grown Horsemen* by Geoffrey Gambado, 1787, stipple engraving, $8\frac{7}{8} \times 7\frac{3}{4}$ in. Private Collection, London

Thomas Rowlandson (1756–1827): *The Duke of Grafton reviewing his Stud*, pen and watercolour, $5\frac{3}{4} \times 9\frac{1}{2}$ in. Collection: Lord Euston, London

116 Théodore Géricault (1791–1824): *Cavalry Officer on Horseback*, 1812, oil on canvas, $22\frac{1}{2} \times 17\frac{1}{8}$ in. Musée du Louvre, Paris (Photo: Giraudon)

Théodore Géricault: *Horses held by Slaves*, oil on canvas, $19 \times 23\frac{5}{8}$ in. Musée des Beaux-Arts, Rouen (Photo: Giraudon)

117 Théodore Géricault (1791–1824): *The Derby at Epsom*, 1821, oil on canvas, $36\frac{1}{4} \times 48\frac{1}{4}$ in. Musée du Louvre, Paris (Photo: Giraudon)

118 Eugène Delacroix (1798–1863): *Study of a Horse*, 26 December 1852, pen and wash, $5 \times 7\frac{3}{4}$ in. From the Collection of Mr and Mrs Paul Mellon, Upperville, Virginia

Jacques-Louis David (1748–1825): *Study of an Antique Horse*, pencil on cream paper, $9\frac{1}{2} \times 13\frac{1}{2}$ in. From the Collection of Mr and Mrs Paul Mellon, Upperville, Virginia

119 Théodore Géricault (1791–1824): *A Grey Stallion*, c. 1815, oil on canvas, $23\frac{1}{2} \times 29$ in. From the Collection of Mr and Mrs Paul Mellon, Upperville, Virginia

120 Jacques-Laurent Agasse (1767–1849): *Bay Ascham, led through a Gate to a Mare*, 1802–4, oil on canvas, $59\frac{3}{4} \times 72$ in. Yale Center for British Art (Paul Mellon Collection), New Haven, Connecticut

121 Jacques-Laurent Agasse (1767–1849): *Study of a Grey Horse*, c. 1800, oil on paper, $8\frac{1}{2} \times 12\frac{1}{4}$ in. From the Collection of Mr and Mrs Paul Mellon, Upperville, Virginia

Henry Bernard Chalon (1770–1849): *A Groom with a Bay Hunter in a Park*, c. 1800, oil on canvas, 40×50 in. Yale Center for British Art (Paul Mellon Collection), New Haven, Connecticut

122 Carle Vernet (1758–1836): *A Mameluke Archer on Horseback*, watercolour, $12\frac{2}{3} \times 15\frac{3}{4}$ in. From the Collection of Mr and Mrs Paul Mellon, Upperville, Virginia

123 Théodore Chasseriau (1819–56): *Hadji Barbary Stallion from the Province of Constantine*, 1853, oil on panel, $24 \times 29\frac{1}{4}$ in. From the Collection of Mr and Mrs Paul Mellon, Upperville, Virginia

Carle Vernet (1758–1836): *A Turkish Groom holding an Arab Stallion*, oil on canvas, 23×28 in. From the Collection of Mr and Mrs Paul Mellon, Upperville, Virginia

124 James Ward, RA (1769–1859): *Colonel Platoff on his Charger*, oil on canvas, 55×43 in. Collection: the Duke of Northumberland, Alnwick Castle, Northumberland (Photo: Paul Mellon Centre for Studies in British Art, London)

James Ward: *A Horse Rolling*, watercolour, $7\frac{1}{4} \times 12\frac{3}{4}$ in. Collection: Mrs R. Gustavus-Jones

125 James Ward, RA (1769–1859): *A Grey Arabian Stallion, the Property of Sir Watkin Williams-Wynne*, c. 1815–20, oil on canvas, 39×49 in. From the Collection of Mr and Mrs Paul Mellon, Upperville, Virginia

126 James Ward, RA (1769–1859): *Portrait of Eagle, the Celebrated Stallion*, 1809, oil on canvas, $35\frac{3}{4} \times 48$ in. Yale Center for British Art (Paul Mellon Collection), New Haven, Connecticut

127 James Ward, RA (1769–1859): *John Levett hunting in the Park at Wychnor*, 1817, oil on canvas, $40\frac{1}{8} \times 50$ in. From the Collection of Mr and Mrs Paul Mellon, Upperville, Virginia

128 John Ferneley Sr (1781–1860): *William Massey-Stanley driving his Cabriolet in Hyde Park*, 1833, oil on canvas, $43\frac{1}{2} \times 62\frac{1}{2}$ in. From the Collection of Mr and Mrs Paul Mellon, Upperville, Virginia

James Pollard (1797–1859): *The Louth–London Royal Mail travelling by Train from Peterborough East, Northamptonshire*, 1845?, oil on canvas, $9\frac{1}{4} \times 12\frac{1}{8}$ in. From the Collection of Mr and Mrs Paul Mellon, Upperville, Virginia

James Pollard: *The Derby Pets: The Arrival*, c. 1842, oil on canvas, $12\frac{3}{4} \times 17\frac{3}{4}$ in. From the Collection of Mr and Mrs Paul Mellon, Upperville, Virginia

129 John Dalby (active 1840–53): *Fox Hunting: Clearing a Bank*, c. 1840, oil on millboard, $5 \times 6\frac{5}{8}$ in. From the Collection of Mr and Mrs Paul Mellon, Upperville, Virginia

Edwin Cooper of Beccles (active *c.* 1820): *A Sportsman with a Shooting Pony and Gun Dogs*, oil on canvas, 25 × 30 in. From the Collection of Mr and Mrs Paul Mellon, Upperville, Virginia

130 John Frederick Herring Sr (1795–1865): *The Greengrocer's Cob*, 1851, oil on canvas, 22 × 30 in. Collection: Richard Green, London

Anson Ambrose Martin (English School, 19th century): *James Taylor Wray of the Bedale Hunt with his Dun Hunter*, 1840, oil on canvas, $20\frac{1}{2}$ × 25 in. From the Collection of Mr and Mrs Paul Mellon, Upperville, Virginia

131 Benjamin Herring (d. 1871): *Silks and Satins of the Turf*, 1865, oil on panel, 20 × $42\frac{3}{4}$ in. From the Collection of Mr and Mrs Paul Mellon, Upperville, Virginia

John Frederick Herring Sr (1795–1865): *The Start of the 1844 Derby*, 1844–5, oil on canvas, $40\frac{1}{2}$ × $80\frac{1}{2}$ in. Brodick Castle, Isle of Arran (Photo: The National Trust for Scotland)

132 Lady Elizabeth Butler (1846–1933): *'Scotland Forever' – The Charge of the Scots Greys at Waterloo*, 1881, oil on canvas, 40 × $76\frac{1}{2}$ in. Leeds City Art Gallery, Leeds

133 Sir Edwin Landseer, RA (1802–73): *The Young Queen Victoria on Horseback*, 1838?, oil on millboard, $20\frac{1}{2}$ × 17 in. Copyright Reserved

134 Edward Troye (1808–74): *American Eclipse*, oil on canvas, 24 × 29 in. From the Collection of The National Museum of Racing, Inc. (Collection: Courtney Burton), Saratoga Springs, New York

135 Edward Troye (1808–74): *Self-portrait*, 1852, oil on canvas, 38 × 54 in. Yale University Art Gallery (Whitney Collection of Sporting Art, given in memory of Harry Payne Whitney and Payne Whitney by Francis P. Garvan), New Haven, Connecticut

William S. Mount (1807–68): *Bargaining for a Horse*, 1835, oil on canvas, 24 × 30 in. The New-York Historical Society, New York

136 Alfred Jacob Miller (1810–74): *Snake Indians*, oil on canvas, $17\frac{1}{2}$ × 23 in. Courtesy of Christie's, London (Photo: Cooper-Bridgeman Library)

137 George Catlin (1794–1872): *A Crow Chief on Horseback in rich Costume*, 1832, oil on canvas, $21\frac{1}{4}$ × 26 in. From the Collection of Mr and Mrs Paul Mellon, Upperville, Virginia

Frederic Remington (1861–1909): *The Cheyenne Buck*, from a series of lithographs, *Bunch of Buckskins*, published in 1901. (Photo: Western Americana Picture Library, London)

138 Jean-Louis-Ernest Meissonier (1815–91): *Sketch for a Figure in a Tricorn Hat on Horseback*, *c.* 1879–85, pen and ink and brown wash heightened with white, $9\frac{3}{4}$ × 7 in. The Pierpont Morgan Library, New York (Photo: Courtesy T. Agnew and Sons, London)

Briton Riviere, RA (1840–1920): *In Manus Tuas Domine*, 1879, oil on canvas, $58\frac{1}{8}$ × $85\frac{3}{4}$ in. The City of Manchester Art Galleries, Manchester

139 Jean-Louis-Ernest Meissonier (1815–91): *Campagne de France, 1814*, 1861, oil on canvas, $20\frac{1}{4}$ × $30\frac{1}{8}$ in. Musée du Louvre, Paris (Photo: Giraudon)

140 René Princeteau (1844–1914): *Chevaux de Course sur la Plage*, oil on canvas, $17\frac{1}{4}$ × $21\frac{1}{2}$ in. From the Collection of Mr and Mrs Paul Mellon, Upperville, Virginia

141 Alfred de Dreux (1810–60): *Retour de la Course*, oil on canvas, $28\frac{1}{4}$ × $35\frac{1}{4}$ in. From the Collection of Mr and Mrs Paul Mellon, Upperville, Virginia

142 Jean-Louis Forain (1852–1931): *Les Courses à Deauville*, watercolour, 18 × $23\frac{3}{4}$ in. From the Collection of Mr and Mrs Paul Mellon, Upperville, Virginia, © SPADEM Paris 1980

James McNeill Whistler (1834–1903): *The Good Shoe*, 1895, lithograph, $6\frac{5}{8}$ × $4\frac{3}{4}$ in. Private Collection, London

143 Eugène Louis Lami (1800–90): *Groom à Cheval*, 1836, watercolour over pencil heightened with white, $7\frac{3}{4}$ × $8\frac{1}{4}$ in. Private Collection, England

Pierre Auguste Renoir (1841–1919): *Riding in the Bois de Boulogne*, 1873, oil on canvas, $102\frac{3}{4}$ × 89 in. Kunsthalle, Hamburg

144 Edgar Degas (1834–1917): *Studies of Horses*, 1866–72?, pencil, 12 × $7\frac{1}{2}$ in. From the Collection of Mr and Mrs Paul Mellon, Upperville, Virginia

Edgar Degas: *Chevaux dans la Prairie*, 1871, oil on canvas, $12\frac{5}{8}$ × $15\frac{3}{4}$ in. Courtesy Durand-Ruel, Paris

145 Edgar Degas (1834–1917): *Thirteen Statuettes of Horses*, wax. From the Collection of Mr and Mrs Paul Mellon, Upperville, Virginia

146 Edgar Degas (1834–1917): *Les Cavaliers*, *c.* 1885, oil on canvas, $28\frac{3}{4}$ × $35\frac{3}{4}$ in. From the Collection of Mr and Mrs Paul Mellon, Upperville, Virginia

Edgar Degas: *Horse with Jockey up*, *c.* 1889, charcoal, $6\frac{3}{8}$ × $9\frac{1}{4}$ in. Collection: Robert Schmit Gallery, Paris

147 Edgar Degas (1834–1917): *Jockeys in the Rain*, *c.* 1886?, pastel crayon, $18\frac{1}{2}$ × 25 in. The Burrell Collection, Camphill Museum, Glasgow (Photo: Cooper-Bridgeman Library)

148 Henri de Toulouse-Lautrec (1864–1901): *Le Tandem*, 1899, black and coloured crayon, 14 × 10 in. From the Collection of Mr and Mrs Paul Mellon, Upperville, Virginia

Constantin Guys (1802–92): *Militaires en Parade*, pen and black wash, 7 × 10 in. From the Collection of Mr and Mrs Paul Mellon, Upperville, Virginia

149 Pierre Bonnard (1867–1947): *Horse's Head*, *c.* 1906, pen and chinese ink, $6\frac{5}{8}$ × $5\frac{1}{8}$ in. Collection: Richard Nathanson, London, © SPADEM Paris 1980

Odilon Redon (1840–1916): *Pegasus*, *c.* 1895, lithograph. Private Collection (Photo: Bulloz)

150 Paul Gauguin (1848–1903): *The White Horse*, 1898, oil on canvas, $55\frac{1}{8}$ × 36 in. Musée du Louvre, Paris

Pablo Picasso (1881–1973): *The Horse*, 1901, ink and crayon, $3\frac{1}{2}$ × $5\frac{1}{4}$ in. From the Collection of Mr and Mrs Paul Mellon, Upperville, Virginia, © SPADEM Paris 1980

151 Pablo Picasso (1881–1973): *Harlequin on Horseback*, 1904, oil on cardboard, $39\frac{1}{4}$ × $27\frac{1}{4}$ in. From the Collection of Mr and Mrs Paul Mellon, Upperville, Virginia, © SPADEM Paris 1980

Franz Marc (1880–1916): *The Yellow Horses*, 1910–11, oil on canvas, $26\frac{3}{8}$ × $41\frac{1}{8}$ in. Staatsgalerie, Stuttgart

152 Robert Polhill Bevan (1865–1925): *The Cab Horse*, 1910, oil on canvas, 25 × 30 in. The Tate Gallery, London

Jack Butler Yeats (1871–1957): *The Squireen*, 1899, watercolour, $13\frac{3}{4}$ × $20\frac{1}{4}$ in. Theo Waddington, London

153 Ben Nicholson (b. 1894): *Rambler 2*, 1977, mixed media on paper, $24\frac{1}{2}$ × $26\frac{1}{2}$ in. Waddington Galleries, London (Photo: Courtesy of the Artist)

154 George Bellows (1882–1925): *Polo at Lakewood*, 1910, oil on canvas, $45\frac{1}{4}$ × $63\frac{1}{2}$ in. Columbus Museum of Art (Art Association Purchase), Columbus, Ohio

Sir Alfred Munnings, PRA (1878–1959): *After the Race; Cheltenham Saddling Paddock*, *c.* 1937, oil on canvas, $40\frac{1}{2}$ × 60 in. From the Collection of Mr and Mrs Paul Mellon, Upperville; Virginia, © The Sir Alfred Munnings Art Museum, Dedham

155 Sir Alfred Munnings, PRA (1878–1959): *Royal Minstrel, owned by John Hay Whitney, with Joe Childs up*, 1929, oil on canvas, $12\frac{1}{4}$ × $16\frac{1}{2}$ in. From the Collection of Mr and Mrs Paul Mellon, Upperville, Virginia, © The Sir Alfred Munnings Art Museum, Dedham

Index

Page numbers in *italic* refer to illustrations

Aesop, *Leben und Fabeln*, 55
Agasse, Jacques-Laurent, 36, 110; *120, 121*
Alexander Sarcophagus, 47
Alexander the Great, 25, 47
American Civil War, 38
American Quarter Horse, 38
Arab horses, 15, 25, 28, 34; *14, 15*
Assyrian art, 23; *43*
Aurelius, Marcus, Equestrian Statue of, 29–30, 49; *29*

Baldung Grien, Hans, *71*
Barb horses, 34
Barberini Ivory, 27
Bayeux Tapestry, 32; *54*
Beckford, Peter, 37
Bella, Stefano della, 32; *80*
Bellows, George, *154*
Bevan, Robert Polhill, *152*
Blake, William, *1*
Bologna, Giovanni (Giambologna), 30; *73*
Bonnard, Pierre, *149*
Il Borgognone (Jacques Courtois), 34
Boultbee, John, 36
Browne, Hablot, 37
Bunbury, Henry, *115*
Burgkmair, Hans, 28; *58*
Burton, Dr John, 35
Butler, Lady Elizabeth, *132*
Byerly Turk, 34

Cambiaso, Luca, 32
Caravaggio, *74*
carriages, 37–8
Catlin, George, 38; *137*
cave paintings, 22; *20*
Chalon, Henry Bernard, 93; *121*
chariots, 23; *12, 49*
Charlemagne, Emperor, 26, 30
Charles II, King of England, 34, 95
Charles V, Emperor, 28, 32; *33*
Chasseriau, Théodore, *123*
Chinese art, 26; *26, 50–2, 84, 87*
Christianity, 26–7
Clouet, François, 33

Colleoni, Bartolommeo, 30
Condé, Duc de, 37
Conquistadores, 22
Constantine the Great, Emperor, 30
Cooper, Abraham, 36
Cooper, Edwin, of Beccles, *129*
Courtois, Jacques (Il Borgognone), 34
Cranach, Lucas, the Elder, 28; *58*
Crimean campaign, 28
Cromwell, Oliver, 28
Crusades, 27–8
Currier, Nathaniel, 38
Cuyp, Aelbert, 32; *82*

Dalby, David, *14*
Dalby, John, *129*
Darley Arabian, 34
David, Jacques-Louis, 33, 36, 38–9; *37, 118*
Degas, Edgar, 39; *40, 144, 145, 146, 147*
Delacroix, Eugène, 39; *118*
Diepenbeck, Abraham van, 34
Donatello, 30, 33; *66*
Doomer, Lambert, *70*
Dreux, Alfred de, 39; *141*
Dughet, Gaspard, 35
Dürer, Albrecht, 26–7, 32; *27, 61, 69*

Eglinton Tournament, 28
Egyptian art, *42*
Elizabeth I, 28–9
English Civil War, 28
Etruscan art, *11, 48*

Falconet, Etienne-Maurice, 33
Ferdinand, King of Aragon, 28
Ferneley, John, Sr, 38; *128*
First World War, 40
Forain, Jean-Louis, 37; *142*
Frederick II, the Great, 28
Füseli, Henry, 35
Fyt, Jan, 35

Gainsborough, Thomas, 35
Garrard, George, 36

Gauguin, Paul *150*
General Stud Book, 34
Géricault, Théodore, 37, 39; *16, 116, 117, 119*
Gilpin, Sawrey, *114*
Giotto, 29
Giovanni di Paolo, *55*
Girardon, François, 33
Giulio Romano, 28, 33; *72*
Godolphin Barb, 34
Gonzaga family, 28, 73
Gooch, Thomas, *108, 110*
Goya, Francisco de, 39
Gozzoli, Benozzo, *59*
El Greco, *74*
Greek art, 25; *12, 24, 25, 44–7*
Grisone, Federico, 34
Gros, Baron Antoine-Jean, 39
Guys, Constantin, 37; *148*

Halicarnassus, horses from, 26; *25*
Haute Ecole, 34, 107
Henderson, Charles Cooper, 38
Henry VIII, King of England, 28, 35
Herculaneum, 47, 118
Herring, Benjamin, *18, 131*
Herring, John Frederick, Sr, 37; *130, 131*
Housebook, Master of the, 55

Indian art, *85, 87*
Ingres, Jean Auguste Dominique, 39
Ives, James 38

Japanese art, *84*
Jockey Club, 34

Lami, Eugène Louis, *143*
Landseer, Sir Edwin, 32, 37; *133*
Leech, John, 37
Le Brun, Charles, *76*
Leonardo da Vinci, 30, 32, 33, 35, 41; *67*
Limbourg brothers, *63*
Louis XIV, King of France, 33
Louis XV, King of France, 34

Manet, Edouard, *19*
Marc, Franz, *151*
Marini, Marino, 40; *41*
Markham Arabian, 34
Marshall, Ben, 36; *106*
Martin, Anson Ambrose, *130*
Martini, Simone, *56*
Mausolus, King, 26
Maximilian I, Emperor, 28
Meissonier, Jean-Louis-Ernest, 39; *138, 139*
Michelangelo, 29; *68*
Miller, Alfred Jacob, *136*
Mongolian ponies, 26; *51*
Montovano, Rinaldo, *73*
Morgan horses, 38
Morland, George, 37
Mount, William S., *135*
Mühlberg, Battle of, 32
Munnings, Sir Alfred, 40, 93; *154, 155*
Muybridge, Eadweard, 39; *145*
Mytton, John, 37

Napoleon I, Emperor of the French, 38, 117; *37*
Napoleonic Wars, 38–9
Newcastle, William Cavendish, Duke of, 34
Nicholson, Ben, *153*

Orléans, Duc d', 39
Orsi, Lelio, *75*
Oudry, Jean-Baptiste, 32

Pagni, Benedetto, *73*
Parthenon, Athens, 25; *24, 46*
Persian art, 23–5; *15, 53, 86*
Peter the Great, Tsar, 22, 33
Phidias, 25
Picasso, Pablo, 40; *150, 151*
Piero di Cosimo, *71*
Pisanello, Antonio, 30; *16, 60, 68*
Pluvinel, Antoine de, 34
Pollaiuolo, Antonio, 30; *66*
Pollard, James, 38; *128*
Princeteau, René, 39; *140*
Przewalski horse, 22

Pytchley Hunt, 35

Quorn Hunt, 35

Raeburn, Sir Henry, *113*
Raphael, 32; *72*
Redon, Odilon, *149*
Reis d'Eisenberg, Baron, 34
Rembrandt van Rijn, *83*
Remington, Frederic, 34, 38; *137*
René d'Anjou, *62*
Renoir, Pierre Auguste, *143*
Riccio, Andrea, 30
Ridinger, Johann, 32, 34; *107*
Rivers, Lord, 36
Riviere, Briton, *138*
Roman art, 23, 29–30; *29, 49*
Rowlandson, Thomas, 38; *115*
Rubens, Sir Peter Paul, 33, 36, 39; *78, 79*
Ruini, Carlo, 35

St Mark's Cathedral, Venice, bronze horses from, *48*
Sakic art, 22; *21*
Sandby, Thomas, 97
Sartorius, Francis, Sr, *106*
Sassanian art, *53*
Savery, Roelant, *70*
Seidlitz, General, 28
Seymour, James, 35; *13, 88, 89, 90, 92, 93*
Sforza, Francesco, 30, 67
Shaw, William, *111*
Siberechts, Jan, 35
Skeaping, John, 40
Snyders, Frans, 35
Standardbred, 38
Stone Age cave paintings, 22; *20*
Stubbs, George, 30, 32, 35–6, 41; *6, 17, 36, 94, 95, 96, 98, 99, 100–1, 102, 103, 104, 105, 109*
Surtees, Robert, 37

Tarpan, 22
Thirty Years' War, 28
Tillemans, Pieter, 35; *91*

Titian, 32, 33, 76; *33, 75*
Toulouse-Lautrec, Henri de, 151; *148*
Troye, Edward, 38; *134, 135*
Turk horses, 34
Tutbury Stud, 29

Uccello, Paolo, 30–2; *31, 64, 65*
Uffington White Horse, *10*

Vanderbank, John, *81*
Van der Venne, Adrien, *81*
Van Dyck, Sir Anthony, 33, 81; *77, 78*
Velasquez, Diego, 32–3; *77*
Vernet, Carle, *122, 123*
Verrocchio, 30, 33
Vix, Great Vessel from, 23; *21*

Ward, James, 36–7, 39; *124, 125, 126, 127*
Wedgwood, Josiah, 36
Wellington,, Duke of, 28
Whistler, James McNeill, *142*
Wootton, John, 35; *93*
Wouwermans, Philips, 34; *82*
Wu, Emperor of China, 26
Wyck, Jan, 34, 35

Xenophon, 34

Yeats, Jack Butler, *152*